GW01606297

The Fisherman The Avatar and GOD

Robert Clayton-Cragg

TO LARRY

WITH LOVE

Published by Dandelion Digital - 2011

13 Grayham Road, New Malden, Surrey, KT3 5HR, UK
E-mail: katy@dandeliondigital.co.uk

Copyright © Robert Clayton-Cragg - 2011

The Author has asserted his moral right
to be identified as the author of this work.

This book is an account of actual events and experiences.
Names, characters, places and incidents have not been changed.

All rights reserved. No part of this publication may be reproduced, stored in a retrieval system or transmitted in any form or by means, electronic, mechanical, photocopying, recording or otherwise, without prior permission of the publishers.

Cover artwork by Mitchell Clayton-Cragg. Photo credit: NASA

ISBN 978-1-908706-00-3

Distributer: Dandelion Digital

An ebook of this title is available from Amazon Kindle

The Fisherman The Avatar and GOD

Ancient wisdom teachings revealed. Beyond 2012.
The Ascension of Humanity and Earth

By Robert Clayton-Cragg

Acknowledgments

Firstly, my five star connection: Joan, George, Ria and Johnny.

My Bulawayo Family of Light: Thelma, Celia, Maude, the Bulawayo Sai Baba Group and the Broomberg Family - in fondest memory of Harold.

To my friend Val, (Amazon woman), without whose inspiration and foresight this book would never have come into being.

To Sathya Sai Baba - Bless you for making me aware of your magnificence.

To my wife, Kim, who lives unconditional love and to my daughter, Carolyn, who knows far more than she realises.

Finally, to all of those not mentioned who have been an inspiration in my life and invaluable in helping me to get this book published and especially my son Mitchell.

Contents

A Reader's Comment

This is a non-fiction account of one man's incredible journey from wartime London, as a small child, to Africa - and back again to the United Kingdom many years later.

Along the way he lived and worked in South Africa and the Rhodesia's - which would later become Zimbabwe and Zambia, for a total of 59 years. In his personal life, he married, divorced, fathered two children, excelled at sport and was a successful businessman.

He always had a great love of nature - which sometimes put him in danger from the likes of crocodiles, hippos and elephant when he ventured into remote areas on fishing and camping trips.

Then, in 1998, he met two people in Johannesburg who changed his life - and helped him in his quest for truth and spiritual enlightenment. It transpired that they were part of a five star Earth connection that were destined to meet up. They had been receiving full trance channelled messages for over 20 years at that stage.

This was the turning point in the life of the author and the culmination of many strange events that had occurred in his life. This fascinating book includes many insights from over 600 channelled messages and information gained by the author during meditations, study of the esoteric and visions.

He left Zimbabwe to return to England in 2003 with no intention of writing a book about his experiences. But, in June 2005, events led him to use the 600 tapes in his possession to write a volume dedicated to bringing the ancient wisdom teachings to a wider audience.

Preface

London 1946

My earliest memories were when I was about 3 years of age therefore they are vague and might be out of sequence. There were loud noises again, which woke me up in confusion, my bed wet again… I'm standing at the doorway of my bedroom, not sure what to do. My mother 'scooped' me up under her arm and hurried downstairs shouting to my sister, 'get in the shelter!' an urgency in her voice. My sister stands in the hallway, confused and sleepy eyed. Mum puts me down at the back door then opens… sirens wailing eerily… search-lights piercing the darkness and shining on the clouds. Mum goes back into the house to get something... my sister stumbles past me into the shelter… I stand alone uncertain what to do, looking up at the tiny red lights going up into the sky in rhythm with the clack-clack-clack of a gun. Then, another loud 'cruu….mp', far away… Mum comes back and says, 'Get in the shelter, Get in the shelter!'I step out-side, it's cold, and wet… I'm holding a blanket - or is it a pillow? My sister is sitting in the corner, eyes wide open staring at us… She is wrapped in a red blanket– strange I thought…a candle burning on a small table next to her.

Time stood still… the cold night air made me shiver… a noise behind me, then Mum picks me up as the air shakes… she trips into the shelter, falling into the corner… The candle goes out… it's dark, I hear my mother breathing heavily, then, fumbling in the darkness, she strikes a match… the smell of sulphur… the candle is lit again…my mother starts singing, and then my sister. 'Army red army, marching into battle, with their guns'...The sirens gradually stop, with only the occasional 'cruu…..mp' of noise in the distance. I smell my mother, something homely, comforting. Where's my dad?....Mummy where's Dad? 'He's working, don't worry go to sleep'. My last memory was the smell of urine and dampness.

Its morning…sun-shine penetrates a gap in the curtains, I'm embarrassed… my side of the bed is wet. I'm in a double bed with my sister, I think? I go downstairs taking my pyjama bottoms off… I'm standing on a chair at the scullery, rubbing my body with a wet cloth. My dad holds me out the window; it's night time, I see searchlights in the sky and far away I hear the noise of bombs… There's a red glow in the sky, Mum says 'That's Hendon getting it… I'll make some tea'. I look up the street to my right… there's a flash near the shop on the corner, so my dad hurriedly pulls me back into the room… 'An incendiary bomb' he say's to Mum, I ask if I can see it… he holds me out of the window again. I see the flames. It's just me, Mum, and Dad - my sisters and brother have gone away? (I was to learn as I grew up, that my brother and sisters were evacuated.) A small coal fire is burning, it's warm and comforting.

Another cold overcast, and drizzly morning. The girl next door and I are playing in the big shelter in the street. She asked me why I was wearing a dress again, I didn't know. We walked up to the shop on the corner as I tell her about last night's events in my usual stuttering manner. Part of the wall is broken, also a big pane of glass and there's lots of water in the shop… A horse drawn vegetable cart arrives and Mum buys me a banana. I've never seen one before and don't know how to eat it. She smiles and peels it for me. An incendiary bomb hit the school over the road last night and the firemen were still putting it out when I went out to play - it was only half burned. We're standing outside in the street - I was older now, about five; everyone is giving the victory sign, smiling, and talking excitedly. My Dad points at the sky; I see a rocket high up, it's silver in colour, Dad said it was a 'doodle bug' and that it was to proclaim the end of the war… I think?

Its 1946, I'm about 5 ½ years old; I remember looking up at a big ship, and being very excited as we climbed the gang-way; streamers were thrown down to people standing at the quayside, some held onto them as the ship slowly moved away, and then they broke. My Mum, brother, and sisters waved goodbye to our family, that had come to see us off; my mother, and sisters were sad, and one of them was crying. My Dad was not with us, and I would learn later that he had left for East Africa before us. We're on the boat, its grey overcast and rainy, and the boat is swaying in the sea, we're all sea-sick, Mum says we're in the Bay of Biscay, that's why the ship is rolling.

I remember that there was a concert on the boat, and my brother singing 'Bless this house', everyone was very impressed. I have clear mental image pictures of these events, and arriving at a place where our boat - the Dominion Monarch, towers above a tiny strip of water.

There are strange dark skinned men in brightly coloured 'dresses' in small boats beneath us, the sun is shining and its warm; they have lots of handbags, and other things on their boats. Ropes are thrown up to us, with baskets attached… there's a lot of shouting - something about 'Gillie men', everyone is smiling and talking to each other. I remembered a beautiful brown handbag that my mother liked; it went up and down in the basket two times, until she bought it, at the price she wanted to pay for it. I thought at the time why don't we just take it, they can't get up here we are far above them; and then I remember thinking, it's nice that people trust each other, it seemed very important to me that people trust each other.

Our ship started sounding its horn, and then there was frenzied activity below, as the boat moved slowly down the narrow waterway; ropes and baskets hurriedly going up and down over the side of the ship. Someone threw some money down to a small boat, but some of it fell in the water, so more money was thrown, but it was hopeless. My last memory was of a basket floating precariously between two small boats.

There was only water from horizon to horizon; it was a lovely warm morning, the sea was a deep blue/green, which met the lighter silvery blue of the sky; a few wispy white clouds, floating in the sky above. There was a lot of activity around the boats swimming pool this morning; someone was about to be thrown into it by a bearded man with a large forked spear, everyone was laughing and happy, so I wasn't worried. It was something to do with the equator, and a man called Neptune.

It occurred to me years later, what a momentous step my father had taken in moving to Africa - the British colonies, with a wife and four children, having only ever known London. I was to remain in Africa for the next 59 years, firstly in East Africa, then South Africa, and finally the Rhodesia's - that would later become known as Zimbabwe and Zambia. Africa would become a part of me, and I a part of Africa; I learnt the ways of Africa, the animals, trees, fauna and flora, the rivers, lakes, and dams, the aquatic life, and rainy seasons, the mood of Africa, and the indigenous peoples. Most of all I would learn that in the remote areas of Africa, I could find calmness and peace that gave me great joy.

The quiet little stuttering Boy who left England was never happier than being alone and at one, with this special country. I would father two children, excel at many different sports, run my own businesses, and make many friends - and a few enemies also, for that is life. I would have many exciting and strange experiences most of which are not part of this book; my life would be threatened by indigenous man during the Congo uprising and the Rhodesian war of independence. I would also have many narrow escapes from some of the animals, because of my love for the remote areas, and numerous fishing and camping trips where crocodiles, hippos, elephant, and lion were not always friendly. I would leave school and work on a bush clearing scheme, for one of the largest dams in the Southern hemisphere - the mighty Kariba dam, on the Zambezi River. Kariba has an average width of 15 miles and is 200 miles long. (About four times larger than Hampshire) I would become involved in animal rescue because many species became trapped in trees, and on islands, as the dam waters rose flooding the Zambezi valley.

I was to have certain experiences in Africa - and in my life generally, that were initially difficult to understand or explain, and a strong sensing that there was more to me than my human mind and physical body. As a young man I had read my Dad's books on the Rosicrucian's, Flying saucers, extra sensory perception, etc. As I grew up, I explored many esoteric paths to try and learn more about the real meaning of life, the soul, and the spirit. I read and re-read the bible, trying to tie-up my innate spiritual knowingness of the real purpose of life; some of these searching's feature within the pages of this book, but there would always be more questions than answers. No sooner had I begun to understand a specific aspect of spirituality or religion, then something else would come up to send me on a further quest for truth.

The culmination of my search for truth began in February 1988, when I met Harold Broomberg who put me in touch with Joan Williams, Amy Kotze, and George Adams - the channel of the Arel centre in Johannesburg. At that time the centre had been receiving full trance channelled messages for nearly 20 years; the full story of this contact will unfold within this book - under The Fisherman chapters, as 'the fisherman' recalled strange events that occurred in his early life, as I discovered that even though I didn't rate myself very high as a member of the human race, all was not what it seemed.

I would ask that the reader considers the unfolding chapters of this book with an open mind, for much is happening now - on earth and in heaven, and we are all involved in it; indeed we are a vital part of a quantum leap into cosmic consciousness, understood as ASCENSION which is in truth TRANSMUTATION of physical matter, into pure spirit. The vast majority of deeper spiritual truths in this book are taken from some of the 600 full trance channelled tapes and also information that came to me during meditations, and many years of study reading. Some of the contents contained within the chapters of this book are searchingly deep and may cause anxiety to certain readers; I must therefore hasten to say that THE FINAL WORD ON TRUTH HAS YET TO BE STATED. The only truth that is immutable is our I AM PRESENCE, WHICH IS ETERNAL, IMMORTAL AND INDESTRUCTABLE.

I would come to know from deep within myself that WE ARE ALL GODS - indeed the bible tells us this in many different chapters and verses; sadly 'the learned ones' have always tried to interpret these teachings, as meaning something else. Amongst the many teachings our beloved master Jesus gave us, he said: 'Things that I do you can do and even greater things'; we know that he transfigured his body into Light, and returned to walk amongst mankind in his ascended human body, and also that he could appear and disappear at will.

This book will give deeper insights into his time on earth 2000 years ago, and in some chapters, I have included some of his teachings, and messages. Also included are many other messages from other entities of those times - some of whom are known to mankind, from our recent history. Communications from THE SONS OF GOD - THE BAI'NOR, whose vast etheric inter universal space craft, come under the control of the creator lords of light – THE ELOHIM. These bio space laboratories are variously described as, miniature worlds, sun discs, mother ships, etc. One such miniature world is our own city of light –SHAMBALLA also known as the 'New Jerusalem'. Shamballa is 'anchored' above the eastern Himalayans mountain's, extending into the Gobi desert. The Tibetan master - Dwaal Khuul referred to it in his Great Invocation as 'the centre of the race of men'. Deep insights into these and other aspects of Spirituality feature strongly within the different chapters. It was given to the Johannesburg group that these communications - understood as THE ANCIENT WISDOM AND MYSTERY TEACHINGS would be at the deepest level, ever given to mankind.

In 2003 I left Zimbabwe for England - the land of my birth - and had no intention of writing a book, but events changed in October 2004. I brought with me over 600 full trance channelled messages that came into my possession, because of my link with a five star group that had incarnated around the same time, to bring the ancient wisdom truths to mankind at this crucial time. Details of this five star link will unfold in the following chapters of The Fisherman. Wherever ***ITALICS*** have been used within the chapters, it denotes full trance channelled messages. An **ASTERIX (*)** is used to highlight certain words that the reader may not be familiar with and are clarified at the end of each chapter.

The Author.

Chapter 1

THE FISHERMAN

My first impressions of Africa were of the large house we lived in, built on a hill overlooking the harbour at Dar-Es-Salaam, and how lovely and warm it was in this new country compared to the cold of England. I recall sitting in the branches of a huge Mango tree eating ripe mangoes and that my Dad was now wearing light brown knee-length trousers which I thought looked strange and made his legs look very funny indeed. He was working on the East African railways as an engine driver, the job he'd been doing in London. I don't remember very much more about Dar-Es-Salaam except that I loved to sit quietly looking down on the harbour at ships and boats moving on the water. These recollections are vague, but I do remember having a friend about my age, and starting a grass fire near to his house; it burnt an area of golf course fairway, and my mother arrived red faced and angry, but I don't think I got a hiding!

One evening my sisters, brother and friends were sitting in the lounge whilst Mum was in the kitchen preparing supper. I was seated in the hallway between them in my own little world. I sensed a strange vibration – an energy of fear, from the lounge, and then the voices suddenly went quiet and I realized they were telling ghost stories. Up until that point I had not really been listening but now the energy had changed and I listened in fascination as the stories unfolded, nervous laughter punctuating the silences.

My fear and awe increased and it felt as if everyone in the lounge was trapped in a vibration of fear. I looked up at a picture my mother had brought with her from the UK, a framed silver cut-out of a ballerina that my sister June had made at school. I thought if that picture falls everyone will get a fright then they'll stop telling ghost stories, my fear will go away, and things will be normal again. Suddenly it did fall smashing on the floor! Someone gasped and my mother rushed into the hallway to investigate. I said 'Mum the picture just fell off the wall by itself!' She picked it up, calling my sisters to sweep up the broken glass.

The atmosphere returned to normal and the broken remains were put on a bookshelf but I knew without question that somehow I had caused the picture to fall. When I was about 6½ years of age we moved to Tabora in Tanganyika. I had not yet been to school so I was sent to a boarding school, at a place called Eldoret. It was all very confusing with no parents, brothers and sisters, just some children I did not know and a strange lady escorting us on the train journey to the school. Arriving in the dark we were led into a large hall, given mugs of cocoa, then taken to our dormitory by our house matron and shown our beds. After my first term at boarding school I returned to a new home at Thompson's falls where my dad joined a company called Marmanet Sawmills as the steam/mechanical engineer. I have wonderful memories of Marmanet and living in a log cabin on the edge of a Cedar forest. Water was brought up to the house in an ox cart from a crystal clear spring near the front of the house where I spent many hours in quiet peacefulness.

Water always attracted me and I was fascinated as the bubbles came up from the depths of the clear water forming a large pond; the ferns and flora surrounding the spring were enchanting - it was a special place, and I often walked there and sat on an old log. There was a dank earthy smell around the spring - an inviting energy that seemed to say, you are safe; I remember my mother saying, 'If you can't find Bob he'll be at the spring'. Whenever I sat there, I sensed I was being watched by a presence in the ferns, and bushes, and if I looked hard enough, I would see something moving, yet I had no fear. Sometimes I felt as if I was watching myself from the ferns, it was a strange feeling.

In 1948 we moved from Tanganyika to South Africa then in 1952 from South Africa to Choma in Northern Rhodesia. Choma was a farming community and within a short while of arriving there, I was sent off to boarding school again. We lived on a farm outside of Choma - adjoining a farm of a friend of mine, called John Stevens whom I had met at boarding school. During the December school holidays we arranged to meet at a dam on our farm boundary to fish and shoot. I got up early, packing sandwiches and a cool drink, then set off through the bush to our rendezvous point about three miles away.

I walked half a mile westwards through a lightly forested area behind our house, reaching a large 'Vlei' (a semi wetland with grass reeds and sometimes a small stream), then three quarters of a mile up the Vlei, then Southwards through another forested area. Keeping the sun to my left, I turned in a westerly direction up another Vlei, knowing the dam would be about three quarters of a mile ahead. I realized very early in life that once I'd looked at a map I could create a mental picture in my mind of where I was going and how long it should take.

It was a lovely time of the year; the rains had begun in mid-November, and the grass was green and low to the ground. I looked for Bowa - a giant edible rain mushroom that often grew on and around huge termite mounds, and were prolific at that time of the year. Storm lilies were coming into flower, and also the beautiful red rain lilies; I bent down to look at one more closely; a huge ball of red, fuzz with small ants feeding on the sticky nectar. It was a special moment that imprinted itself on my mind, I felt joy and transfixed by nature's incredible beauty, then I pressed on towards the dam, and then something changed within, or without me.

The air was vibrant, and the sun was warm; a gentle breeze blew, and there was movement everywhere, the colours were clear and brilliant. The birds, butterflies, and insects busy in flight, seemed to be celebrating the beginning of the rainy season. I crested a large rounded termite mound in the middle of the Vlei and to my surprise, saw five Reedbuck about thirty yards in front of me. They just stood looking at me - one male and four females; dark brown fur vivid against the short green grass. Why had they no fear of me, Reedbuck are secretive and skittish, and always run away as soon as they see anyone, but not these? How close they were - snouts shiny and moist and their deep brown/blue eyes, staring at me.

Crouching on one knee I focused on the female in the centre, aiming just behind her shoulder. I squeezed the trigger hearing the crack of the rifle. Dropping the barrel slowly I got up to claim my un-missable prize….. but there was nothing there? How could that be? The Vlei was wide and free of shrubbery and the grass no more than twelve inches high. I walked slowly forward certain there was a dip in the ground; perhaps they had crouched down and would run at any moment? It was barely ten seconds since I'd pulled the trigger, yet there was no donga! This is crazy, I thought, they couldn't just disappear? I did a thorough search but found nothing, it made no sense! I walked slowly up the Vlei to the dam but kept glancing back to the spot where I'd shot the female Reedbuck. John was waiting for me on the dam wall. 'What did you shoot?' he asked. I tried to explain what had happened but he stared at me in disbelief, so I dropped the subject.

We spent the rest of the morning fishing and trying to shoot some wary duck that stayed a good 100 yards away then we walked along the boundary of our farms hoping to shoot a Duiker, but no luck! Returning to the dam we found a shady tree, ate lunch and spent the rest of the day fishing. We caught a few small bream and John got broken-up by a large Barble that stripped the line from his reel. We parted, arranging to see each other at the movies on Friday night. I walked home past the spot where I'd shot at the Reedbuck, double-tracking and searching for spoor. I walked to the ant-hill and measured the distance by stride from a small dead stump that had been on their left, a distance of about 20 yards - it was all very puzzling. This incident has remained with me all my life and is as clear now, as it was at the time. I came to realize over the years, that on that day, I was so much in at-one-ment with nature - as had happened before and would happen again, that I had somehow 'crossed the veil' linking with, the nature kingdoms. I now know that I had viewed the etheric realm of the nature kingdoms - god's creation!

In December 1954 we drove to Ndola for a family Christmas reunion, with my mother's sister, Auntie Alice and Uncle Bob. My Mother's birthday was on Christmas day, and my parent's Wedding Anniversary, was on Boxing Day, so celebrations usually began on Christmas Eve and culminated on Boxing Day. These gatherings were always very noisy; being a musical family, we played bongo drums, the piano accordion, the Melodica, accompanied by loud vocals. Our neighbours were more than happy to be invited, and coupled with an abundance of alcohol; there was much fun and merriment! On that particular Christmas Eve everyone was partying, it was a warm cloudless night, as I walked outside feeling the need to be alone. I remember looking up at the bright stars, through the branches of trees, then moving to the front of the house near the road, where there was nothing to obstruct my view. I looked back towards the house listening to the noise, and laughter, then upwards again at the night sky, ablaze with stars. The milky-way stretched like a silver river across the sky.

A light suddenly surrounded me...... I looked up in surprise but the light did not emanate from above, it just seemed to form an ovoid around me. I was not afraid, but it seemed that time stood still. I felt very calm, and the light seemed natural, and comforting; I was surrounded in an aura of peace, and light, and then suddenly! I became aware of the darkness again, and the stars above me.

I was surprised yet excited, at what had occurred, but instinctively knew it was pointless to tell anyone in the house, what had happened to me - they would not understand. The encircling light had vanished as quickly as it manifested; on recall, the whole event took about seven or eight seconds. Eventually I returned to the house to get a coke from the kitchen, but felt drawn outside again to the same spot - which I did, trying to will the light to encircle me again, but it did not.

On leaving school I joined a bush clearing company working on the Kariba dam hydro-electric project in the Sinazongwe basin, about eighty miles from Choma. One afternoon I was relaxing over tea with my friend Phil, in our new camp on the edge of a thickly forested area. We were discussing whose turn it was to shoot fresh meat, when I jumped up pointing to a bright silver/green object that was arcing slowly over the sky. Phil had his back turned, but seeing the reflection in my glasses leapt up, but the object had disappeared behind the tree line. He asked what I'd seen; I explained that there had been a silver disc with a green shimmering halo, extending around and behind it, and as it headed silently across my field of vision, from right to left. Phil said he had seen the silver/green reflection in my glasses, and it transpired that many of the workers, also observed the object. It became the topic of conversation for some time; interestingly, it transpired that the workers had seen many such objects since the bush-clearing scheme started, and often at night-time?

For the next thirty years I was caught up in playing the game of life; marriage, children, fishing and sport, interspersed with an unquenchable search for deeper truths that would see many esoteric and paranormal books pass through my hands covering a vast array of subjects. During this period I had a number of experiences involving déjà vu, synchronicity, clairvoyance and telepathy; it was also not unusual for me to suddenly think about someone who I hadn't heard from or seen for years and that person would phone out of the blue, or turn up at the gate. Sometimes I would be drawn to phone or call on someone only for them to respond 'Oh we have just been talking about you'.

These events happened far too frequently to be coincidental and became a joke and a talking point with my friends. I also became aware that relative strangers who had problems in their lives would be drawn to confide in me, sharing things they would not normally tell anyone else. Many re-occurring dreams would come to me in my sleep state and remain clearly etched on my mind: one of them would be clarified on a visit to Egypt years later. Looking back it seems that from an early age I was receiving wake-up calls about my real Being-ness and Divinity, but like most people I was very much in the moment and didn't place great significance on them. I became interested in the Rosicrucian organisation, and also read everything from the society of Psychical research, gaining more knowledge on my spiritual path. I also studied Scientology for a short while but at that time could not afford to continue with the courses.

In 1988 I met up with two important people - Harold Broomberg and Joan Williams who would be the catalyst that tied-up many loose ends in my spiritual searching, and would set me firmly on the path to enlightenment. Harold Broomberg, his wife Silvia, and their daughters, had run the Gwaai river hotel for many years. The 'Gwaai' was situated about halfway between Bulawayo and the Victoria falls and was a well-known stopping off point for those going to or coming back from the Zambezi river, the Victoria falls, Whange national game park, and the Western half of lake Kariba.

The 'Gwaai' was a historical landmark from the early days when Southern Rhodesia was a fledgling nation and one of two possible night stops that provided accommodation facilities when travelling between Bulawayo and the North/West of Rhodesia which would later become Zimbabwe. Harold and I were to develop a close friendship during my many stop overs at the 'Gwaai' on fishing trips or business calls.

It was Harold who would eventually introduce me to Joan. Harold and his wife Sylvia were about 65 years of age at that time. Harold was small and stocky with grey hair and when in his company an air of calm pervaded the atmosphere which was enhanced by his gentle soft communications. Never in my 20 years of knowing him, did I ever encounter anger annoyance or frustration that might have been the norm in running a rural company under trying circumstances in Zimbabwe at that time. In addition to the hotel they also ran the petrol station, a small store catering for the local population, and a herd of cattle and sheep for his butchery. Sylvia was fairly short and stocky with grey hair and glasses. She was friendly and business like and was always moving between the kitchen bar and reception office in addition to keeping an eye on the cleaning and bedroom room staff. Their daughter Louise was slim with dark short hair and a mischievous smile.

Weekend evenings at the Gwaai were always party time for the isolated hunters and farmers in that area. Harold would get on the 'tea chest' bass and a local rancher or hunter's wife would get on the piano (or whoever was passing through), and I would play my guitar. These parties often finished well into the early hours and local hunters or farmers liked to be advised if I was coming up on a fishing trip. Initially Harold and I chatted about fishing and other subjects and I found him to be a very caring and genuine person; he made strong but searching eye contact with me, it was as if he knew something about me that I did not.

During one of my fishing trips to Olive Beadle fishing camp on Lake Kariba, I stopped at the Gwaai for brunch and petrol, Harold joined me for tea. During our conversation he said, 'Why don't you stop over on your way back from fishing'? I agreed, sensing that we both wanted to learn more about each other. I returned to the Gwaai on Friday afternoon ordered tea and was joined shortly by Harold and Louise who enquired about the fishing - which had been good. I suggested we have a few bream for supper. Louise excused herself and Harold casually handed me an audio tape to listen to, suggesting I play it before supper as he would be interested in my comments; it was by Ram Das, an American who had found his spiritual meaning to life in India.

The tape was interesting but different; we discussed it and other esoteric thoughts and philosophies and it seemed we had similar thoughts about God and spirituality generally. His daughter Louise - who was managing the Gwaai at that time, joined in on our discussions and I was to learn that her path was with The Emissaries of Divine Light. The next morning at breakfast Harold handed me three more tapes explaining that they were full trance channelled messages from a Light channel centre in Johannesburg. He said I could drop them off, the next time I passed through.

Harold explained to me that the tapes were from a spiritual group in Johannesburg, called the Arel Centre. A few days later - whilst tidying the workshop, I put one of the tapes on, it was entitled, Light Channels. A being called Johnny was talking; I was fascinated by what he had to say, it was as if I knew this being called Johnny, and could almost anticipate his next words, a strange but exciting feeling. I was later to learn, that I was listening to an old friend from a previous dispensation of time, (from the other side of the veil) a soul being whom I'd known in previous lifetimes, and part of my soul family group. I resonated very strongly with what Johnny said, and re-played the tape, hearing deeper things, that I'd somehow missed the first time around.

I played the second tape by Johnny entitled 'After death transition', and then listened to the third tape, by a being called Ra ab Houtep whose topic was, 'The path of light'. I was hearing things that I knew to be pure Truth, and the messages resonated deep within me, even though I did not have total understanding, of all the subject matter. I phoned Harold within the next few days, thanking him for the tapes, and saying how much I'd enjoyed them; I pointed out that I had a deep knowingness of the contents. He said, 'I thought they'd interest you'. I told him my rep was going up to Whange on a business trip, and would drop the tapes off. I asked if he could loan me some more tapes, which he promised to do; He said I think you should make contact with a friend of mine - a lovely lady, called Joan

Williams. He gave me her telephone number and I phoned Joan the next day; she sounded delightful, and we arranged to meet that afternoon at her house.

I was warmly welcomed, as we sat down for tea in her lounge. Joan was a gentle person about 60 years of age, slim, and with short blond silver hair; she had a mischievous smile, and had been married to Rod, for over 40 years. Their house was in the suburb of Matseumshlope on the outskirts of Bulawayo; a large corner house of about one and a half acres, with sprawling gardens. I was to learn that Joan loved her garden, and would often be found pottering around or organizing her gardener. There was instant affinity between us, as we shared our spiritual paths; Joan's paths had been far more active than mine, Yoga, the School of truth, and the Emissaries of Divine Light. Joan also had a large library, known as the Open Circle library, which comprising books covering many spiritual paths, and philosophies; in addition, she had a large range of audio and video tapes.

Many of her books and tapes, had come from the USA, and the UK, it seemed she had many contacts, world-wide. Her path for the last 20 years had been with The Emissaries of Divine light - an American group, that Harold's daughter Louise belonged to. Joan was head of the E.D.L. in Bulawayo and had been to E.D.L. seminars in America, with her husband Rod. She had also spent time at Findhorn, which we discussed in depth; I had recently finished reading a book called the Magic of Findhorn, which was about the nature kingdoms, which I strongly related to. Her stories about their time there, was fascinating, but the afternoon ended too quickly, and I had to get back to work. Joan leant me some books, and I promised to keep in touch.

My marriage was over, and there was the usual unpleasantness, accusations, and counter accusations, in the middle of the whole 'shimos', I lost Joan's contact details. I made a number of efforts to try to locate her house from memory of my first visit, but it was hopeless. Harold was in South Africa, and Louise was away in America, so I could not contact them, and didn't know anyone else who knew her. I drove out to her suburb many times, and eventually - four months later, when travelling that way to look at a boat for sale, I finally recognized the house. I hooted at the gate, and was let in by her gardener. Joan met me on the veranda and said, 'I wondered what had happened to you'? I explained the problems that I'd had, and then over tea, we discussed general spiritual subjects. It seemed we had a lot in common, and I was strongly drawn to her smiling and friendly personality. She invited me to her regular Thursday evening attune-ment meetings; an Emissary technique of honouring and healing the body and spirit. I met her friends, who were also Emissaries; they were lovely people, and the evening passed too quickly. Apparently her group had been together for nearly 15 years, and during that time they had explored Yoga, and were involved with the school of Truth. They were interested in my path, and I was made to feel very welcome.

I continued receiving tapes from Harold who was now back from South Africa. I listened to them enthralled knowing they were re-awakening deep spiritual things within me. Harold had many tapes from the Arel centre with many different beings communicating. He told me that he had visited the centre and that Johnny, the entity who opened the channelling in the late sixties, had come through and spoke to him. It was a continuing joy to listen to Johnny's communications; his humour and winding-up of the group, interspersed with a sometimes serious lesson, and then, a sudden light hearted humorous interaction with them. It was as if Johnny and I were on the same wavelength, I thought with amusement, my friend Johnny's a spook!

Harold invited me up to the Gwaai again. I jumped at the chance to fish in a local dam, and the Gwaai River, and in between times, to share deeper things with him when his work load permitted. I met his other daughter Denny, who was visiting from America. She was also on a strong spiritual path, with the Lazaris group in America. Harold had also lent me some of this great entity's tapes. During the evening we had supper, then retired to the bar; I had brought my guitar with me, and when the local farmers and hunters came in, it was party time again, with musical assistance from a visitor who had night-stopped and played the piano-accordion.

On Sunday morning Harold arranged for tea on the veranda of my room and during our sharing I asked him about the Johannesburg Light centre. He told me his sister-in-law had once been a member of the group and had copied the tapes and sent them to him over the years, then added, 'for some unknown reason she was asked to leave the group and was very annoyed about it'. I re-affirmed my deep link with Johnny and said that I would like to meet George - the channel, and Amy who was the main questioner. He gave me their telephone number and I phoned them the following Monday evening. Amy answered the phone, and after a brief introduction said I was welcome to call on them when down that way suggesting I phone them a few days before a visit. It didn't take me long to find a reason to visit Johannesburg and arranging to stay with a friend, I arrived two months later in a state of anticipation.

I phoned Amy and we agreed to meet the next day at 3.00 pm. George gave me the directions and as Johannesburg is a huge city I left early in case I got lost - which I did, but still made it on time. George met me at the gate and we sat in his flat having tea; he was a slim small man with greying hair, a neat 'goatee' beard and about 65 years of age, with sparkling blue eyes. Amy was apparently visiting her daughter, and would meet me later.

I felt very comfortable with George, and he began telling me how the channelling had started, when suddenly he closed his eyes, and put his hand up to his head, and said, 'Oh you were in Egypt….. You were responsible for some of the hieroglyphs being carved….. You knew the deeper meaning of what was carved on them'…… we know each other', he opened his eyes smiling boyishly at me. I commented on his American accent, but he laughed and said 'Actually Bob I'm from Canada'. He asked if I would like to see the sanctuary where the channelling took place. As we got up he swayed a little, then held on to his arm-chair……. he closed his eyes turning away from me, then steadied himself against the chair, he said 'Sorry Bob just hold on abit, I have a problem with Meniere's disease'. I involuntarily held up my hands radiating light to him; after a short while he straightened up and said, 'thank you for the light that you sent to me'. How did he know I had done that? I was amazed.

We proceeded to the sanctuary which was between Amy and George's living quarters, and I was immediately conscious of a calm and serene vibration and energy. There were six chairs to the left and a large comfortable upright chair with a microphone in front of it –

obviously George's chair where the channelling took place, and two armchairs on the right next to George's chair. Next to this was a chair, and a small table that had a tape recorder on it, I realized immediately that this was Amy's chair.

We sat down and the conversation changed as to how I had met Harold; we had no sooner started when Amy called from the kitchen apologizing profusely for being late due to traffic problems. She walked in and glanced at George, who nodded his head - something had passed between them? She looked at me smiled and said welcome Bob, I'm sorry I wasn't here to meet you I had to take my daughter to the doctor. Amy was short, stocky and motherly with short dark greying hair, and a slightly reserved demeanour. She spoke quietly with an English/Afrikaans accent staring intently at George or myself when we spoke.

I told them of my meeting with Harold and my affinity with Johnny and the messages on the tapes, a knowing smile passed between them again. Amy suggested we sit on the veranda then excused herself to bring some refreshment. George and I continued talking about Johnny, Amy returned a short while later with coffee and rusks. They were interested in my path to spirituality so I told them of things that had happened when I was younger and about the books that I'd read, and finally of my meetings with Joan, and Harold. We shared many things, but as it was getting dark and George was looking tired. I excused myself, anxious not to get lost on the way home. Amy promised to send me some tapes and said that we should stay in touch. I received 28 tapes about two weeks later, and re-listened to them many times, gaining great insight into the ancient wisdom teachings.

I was intrigued about how full trance channelling worked because I had read many books by the Rosicrucian's and other books about medium circles and psychic messages but these full trance channelled messages were very different, and seemed to be of a question and answer communication. There were no 'spooky type' innuendos or vague references to the subject matter, or how Aunty so and so was keeping. Mundane day to day questions from the group by the entity communicating in the early days were often ignored as unimportant and in some instances dis-encouraged! The beings often pointed out that the group should meditate on the information being given and if further clarification was needed it could be brought up at the next channelling. At this juncture I feel it important to give the reader information on full-trance and other types of psychic, medium communications.

Full-trance Channelling, Mediums, Psychics, etc.

For thousands of years man has been spoken to by God, or other entities, from the Astral or spiritual realms. These communications have variously been described by the person experiencing them, as being filled by the holy breath, being light or god filled, or being filled by Spirit, etc. Spiritual or paranormal activities, involve people having visions, hearing voices, having altered states of consciousness, or being out of body, etc. Some communications originate from cosmic Divine mind entities within Universal, Galactic, and Solar, spiritual realms.

Generally speaking, some of these communications- from the other side of the veil, depends on each channel level of human mind, or spiritual, enlightenment. Those who are only concerned with the sensational human mind earth scene, will often receive low level earth/astral information, which are passed on to them, at various levels of purity and truth, via psychics, medium's, etc. I am not suggesting that all Psychic or medium communications are low level, but many of them contact people on the lower astral planes, and earth planes.

Full-trance channelling has come to the fore during the past 70 years, as the Brotherhood of Light seek to enlighten us as to our true origins - our I AM PRESENCE, and the ancient wisdom or mystery teachings. In the case of full-trance channelling, the being or entity communicating, uses the channel as an instrument - or mouth piece, as one entity is often humorously given to say. The 'being' communicates by thought, (telepathy) after the channel has gone into a trance-like state of deep sleep; in this state the channel's human mind is out of the way, and the being or entity using the body, is able to impart their communications to the person or group, without the channel's conscious human mind assessment, or interference. The being impresses the channel's soul mind that it wishes to communicate; thereafter the channel often becomes tired, and eventually falls asleep, at which point the communication begins.

During channelling a being may have problems trying to communicate its pure thought communication, using the channel's mind. Sometimes the channel may not have full understanding of their chosen language, or the correct terminology to use in explaining the thought communication that is being given. One entity - who became a regular communicator with the Arel group, said; ***You would be amazed at what comes out of the channel's mind, which is not what we communicated.'***

JOST - one of the ascended masters from Shamballa, came through for the first time on the 24/6/1982, he said; ***It is a privilege to be together...... let us leave earth things behind, as we share things together. I would like to talk with you, and perhaps to bring in ideas that will perhaps...... more you..... to understand, in your world transpiring....... Oh, the words.......... Jost is not accustomed in this way to talk.*** (Using a channel) ***You must lose the obs..... umm,...... become obscure in your vision of the whole. You must forgive me. I am not with you..... familiar with this........***(Channelling) ***And the language is strange, do you follow, am I clear?***

When the entity communicates, the channel's soul is on standby - so to speak, yet linked to the body as an observer. The channel or instrument, often gets a mental image picture of the subject matter being discussed, in addition to the telepathic communication. Many ethical full-trance channel communications in magazines, or books, wisely tell their readers that they should use discretion on information given within a specific channelling. This is wise counsel because of the afore mentioned problems, The reader should also be aware that the negative powers have their own channels, sowing misinformation; it's a question of using our intelligence, and intuitive censing faculties, to sort out the chaff from the wheat. I hope that the above information on full-trance channelling, will help the reader in greater understanding of what has hitherto become a taboo subject, of fear and misinformation. During the past 40 years, more and more, full trance channel centres have opened up worldwide, giving humanity communications at the highest levels of Love, Light, and Truth.

During this first visit to Amy and George, he related the following story, as to how his channel work had started; 'Around 1967 a group of us used to meet once a week, to discuss and share views on spirituality, God, and our real purpose for being on earth. Sometimes we read from the bible or other esoteric literature that was brought along by our friends. At that stage we were working mainly as Christians because we all had incredible love for Jesus; when some other viewpoint was raised, heated debates were the order of the day, we look back now and laugh about it.

One evening I fell asleep in the middle of a reading by one of the group. I woke up apologizing for my rudeness then realized that everyone was staring at me in a strange way? Amy said to me, George you didn't fall asleep, your eyes were open and the voice of a young man was talking to us through you, it was definitely not your voice. George laughed and told them he must have been talking in his sleep, but realised that they didn't seem convinced.

The incident was forgotten and then about three weeks later the same thing happened again; on waking up George was very confused and a discussion took place as to what the young boy had said. It seemed that those present could not agree on the exact communication, so just in case it happened again, they would record the message, and play it back to George. George made it clear that it would not happen again, because he would make sure that he did not fall asleep again. He pointed out that it was obviously a childhood memory that he was recalling, and when he fell asleep he was talking about those memories, but once again the group were not convinced. Nothing happened for the next few months, and their regular weekly meetings continued as before. Then one evening it happened again, but this time Amy recorded what the young boy was saying, and also asked a few questions. She said, 'are you a friend of George, and where do you know him from'? The young man said, ***'I'm Johnny, tell him I knew him from school, he is a teacher'***. George woke up and the tape was played to him, he said, 'Bob I was very confused it didn't make sense, and then I thought, maybe it was a past memory or something'.

The channelling continued, but George wasn't comfortable with what was happing. He told the group to tell Johnny that he had no right to take control of his body, and that it was against his wishes; tell him also that I do not know of a 'Johnny' from school. Another channelling occurred during which Amy put George's questions to Johnny, who said; ***Remind him of a time when it was raining heavily....... He was standing in the doorway of the gymnasium when a little boy came running in from the playing fields, and careered into him.*** George listened to the communication and unthinkingly said, ***Oh! that was Johnny.......... but he died?*** He said; Bob I felt very cold and uncomfortable, because Johnny had passed on years earlier. Johnny was dead, how could he talk through me, from beyond the grave!

Amy put George's fears to Johnny during the next channelling, and Johnny said; ***The channel and I have been together in past lives and are close friends, working for the light, and so are you Amy. George wanted to be a channel in this incarnation - by soul agreement; even as I talk now, George's higher consciousness is nodding its head, in agreement. Tell the teacher that any stage he is uncomfortable with what is happening to him, his human mind is powerful enough to stop the channelling. If he does not want this to happen - to be a channel for the light, tell him it's up to him.***

George decided to go on leave to his family in Canada, in the hope that things would settle down, and allow him to think about what was happening in his life. After his return to Johannesburg, the full trance channelling meetings started in earnest, and George resigned himself to what was happening to him. The group met on Thursday evenings, but channelling also occurred on Sundays, usually only with Amy present. Many years were to pass, and slowly a nucleus within the group realized the deep truth of what was being given by many other entities of the light. A few people in the group saw the channelling as sensationalism, doubting that what was occurring was truth. The spiritual gatekeeper of the group realized that this was causing disharmony, so Amy had the difficult task of sorting out the chaff from the wheat. The group eventually stabilized with five ladies. Over the ensuing years they continued to receive incredible teachings from many different entities.

About four months after my first visit to Amy and George, I phoned them promising to call in on my way through to Durban on holiday. I spent the afternoon in their company, and as I was leaving, Amy suggested I should night-stop with them on my return journey. I had a quiet and peaceful holiday in Durban - needing to be by myself following my divorce, but all the time I was 'chomping at the bit' to get back to Johannesburg. I phoned them the night before my departure, and told them to expect me around 1 pm. I was very excited, and once again I had difficulty finding the freeway turn-off, but I eventually got there.

They expressed delight at seeing me again then Amy showed me to my room, which was next door to the sanctuary. We sat on the veranda and had a light lunch and then - as they usually had a rest in the afternoon, we retired to our rooms. I rested for a short while but my mind was too active so I walked around the garden and sat by a small fish pond with running water. I remembered listening to two messages where running water was audible in the background and realized that this must be the place. George and Amy joined me and we sat on the veranda talking. I gave them more information about Joan's spiritual path, but noticed that George was very fidgety, and seemed tired again. I assumed his Meniere's was causing problems. I also noticed that Amy kept looking at him, and eventually, she suggested we go into the sanctuary.

As George left us to get a jersey, Amy said to me, 'My dear, don't worry if you see George shaking, just sit quietly, it will be okay'. We sat quietly until George returned; he winked at me then sat in his chair. Amy turned the tape on and George's head fell slowly forwards, his right arm began shaking, then he exhaled very deeply, his body very calm. **'He'** raised his head, and opened his eyes.

The following is a transcript of the communication from Johnny, to Joan and my-self, dated the 20/11/92; ***Hello, greetings and blessing, welcome yes, welcome. Right! so we make a contact, good, we will do some talking tonight***.

Amy: Wonderful for you to come down; ***Welcome Bob, yes I told you I was on my way passing through.***

Bob: Thank you so much. ***It's spanning the ages you know that. It's going back a long, long time ago, and if you take a***

really good breath, you might even smell the river of the Nile….. you never know. It's not the first time we've all talked together, we've done this before on a number of occasions. Oh thank you. Joan! Good, thank you…… You brought your friend in you see. (I had just been thinking, I wish Joan could be here with us) ***Joan…… good welcome. She's here too you see; you don't have to have the eyes and the human body to see things and people, you know that don't you, Bob?***

Bob: Yes I do. ***Right, this is an important step that is opening up the work – the light channel work here and, since it was initiated, there's been much given and revealed - and now comes the opening of the door. The work that has been accumulated is now ready for re-channelling - that's actually why I came tonight, because having coordinated it in the beginning - which is what our task was, it's nice to just ride herd on this for a while. We're no strangers… Yes? I know you've heard the tapes, and made contact through my brother,*** (George, the channel)- ***through the voice element that I use with him. That means we are not strangers.***

Bob: Yes, I feel I know you so well. ***Yes that's right. Even in this human life, we are not strangers… and even further back than that; we've had an association - along with others…… Yes Joan, do you want to move closer? ….. Right move in closer, make yourselves a triangulation, and I'll triangulate with you, this is as it should be. If you wish we can talk or answer some questions – there might be one or two, I see a few things buzzing around you, it must be questions, like bees looking for their hive.***

Bob: Yes, the first tape I ever heard came through with you talking. I felt such an affinity - a strong attraction, can you tell me something about that, Johnny? ***Well yes, that goes back - umm….. Now I've got to start trying to work things out in your time, haven't I? It really only goes back a little bit in your time; let's talk about time again, you know that it doesn't exist? Before all of us here, returned to this current life experience – the five of us, we discussed our plans for this incarnation.***

We met on the fifth plane of consciousness, and had a discussion. We knew that each one of us would choose a different role to play and that we would eventually be together in one place as light channels, to root the light. They really had to go and get us from far and wide; they had to pull us in from all over the world - my brother (the channel) ***away from the Eskimos, and you, from far places, to bring us together in a vital area on your planet, in these times. All thinking, both negative, and positive, is focalizing here, because from here will come the concept of unity within diversity, which the whole world is looking for. There are many who have been brought into this Southern African area; with you four particularly - since you incarnated with me, we form the five pointed star, and that is the symbol which will keep us together. I'm not coming back into regular communication by the way.***

Amy: Yes I've often wondered how the messages were going to go out from here, it's a perfect answer. ***Well you did put it in mind didn't you? It goes out from here and gets blessed on its way to the right people, where it will find a response..... The right ones are ready to chew through it; they are really going to chew through it and come up with different explanations than you have – you and my brother Amy, but that doesn't matter, because the truth is the truth. We bless you Bob - you and Joan, as you will seek to be steward custodians of..... this message, as it goes to you. Good you'll enjoy it, and as you've discovered it ties up with so many other messages, doesn't it?***

Bob: Yes, this is the wonderful thing. ***Yes, it's not just uniqueness in that sense. So - to get back to where I went off the rails just now, we had a conference together deciding we would like to form part of a nucleus group - as others have done also in your world. Others also make these little decisions and have their conferences before they incarnate; then one comes ahead of the other to get a few things sorted out, then the next one comes. I was the last one of our group to come into incarnation, as you know; it wasn't so much that I wanted to keep an eye on you, it was just that I had to get the pulse of what was happening with the others, and then we came into line. I was***

able to come down to undergo an Earth experience again to fill in some of the gaps from previous incarnations, and then return to the inner planes, to work with you.

So I was the last to come down, but the first to go back. Anyway, the work continued and that's why you felt an affinity, because we met in the temple garden of the fifth plane deciding we would like to do this. We've been together before in different life experiences, and different places, doing different things, so we know each other, one another.

Bob; I felt it so strongly. ***Well when each one of you met the other, you all knew it, and when I first came to my brother, he knew it also.***

Amy; When I met him, I felt it, and when I met Bob, I also felt it. ***Yes it's because we are a five star triangulation,…. very powerful too. Your work, as you move within this context, will be very strong indeed. We bless you in this next move forward, as the message goes out a bit further again. Right! Now, the next one.***

Bob: Umm ……. so obviously Joan and I had to meet as well, because I felt very strongly drawn to her when we met. ***Yes that's right, and we may well all meet together again, in which case I'll be there in the midst of you…… but it's not that important. What is important is your work, which brings you to the source - as a light centre, which draws the light, and from which the light emanates. You vibe in and meet, and have your physical contact, but that's not as important as your work, you know this. Right, and Joan nods her head, she knows this also. Now we bless your path as it lies before you, however it opens up in love, light, truth, and harmony, right?***

In your land you take an active part in its spiritual growth, in nice quiet ways; it is the working in the secret place of the most high love and wisdom, where the great power work is done, and into the market place with it too. There will be few that will be able to share with you of course. The more sacred part of your work must always be kept in the secret place of the most high love and wisdom, always. There will be few that will be able to share the true sanctity of the message of love and light with you,

so one discriminates as to how much any given person is able to absorb.

Bob: I wonder if you could throw any light on the time I was by the Nile. I have memories of sand and an affinity there. Is it possible for you to tell me something if I allow you to look at this? ***Yes, you had many experiences – this goes for all of us now all together, in ancient Egypt, even before the recorded history of that land. When the Atlantian dispensation culminated/terminated, you decided along with a number of others, that you did not want to perpetuate the errors which brought that civilization to its destruction; so a band of you, a lot of you, US, settled in what was then a newly formed valley with the river of life*** (the Nile)***running through it.***

Up until that time the river had flowed in another direction to another ocean; then the upheavals of the planet were such that it changed its course into its present flow, where it is now. So isolated was this early community that you were able to be trained in perfect purity, and innocence, and were able to grow and be trained in the energies of a new dispensation. You were part of the early innocent communities that lived along the Nile - perhaps very primitive in some ways, but spiritually they weren't primitive. Spiritually they were very enlightened; there was a core of light channels being trained amongst the ordinary people, who were reincarnating into that land...... and you - all of us, had specific training in these temples, especially for the days we are living in now.

So you have gone through the whole gamut of it. Our two great periods together – if I can sort them out one from another, were in the great 18th dynasty, and later on in following dynasties, when we were also together. You have had to undergo the disciplines of training, and initiation, into priesthood. There have been times when you have succeeded in your examinations, and times when you haven't..... thats been true for all of us. When we had succeeded and moved on one step, we had to repeat that step again, until we got it right, and then we entered a higher stage.

Amy: In what capacity was he in the 18th dynasty, if I may ask? ***Near the beginning in the time of the early Tut Mosis, you were in a military capacity, in the armies of the first Amen Houtep, and then the second Tut Mosis; you were related to the Pharoahnic house that's why you held that position…… a high position,…… you were also there Joan. You were trained during that period to learn to rule, then it was awhile before you came back, but you did not come back in a military capacity. You came back into the temple in the time of Amen Houtep the third; it was in the great temple of Karnak, that you had you priesthood office. You were in the priesthood of Amun, the god Amun; you supervised much of the building of Karnak, the part which was raised by Amen Houtep the 3rd. Then you joined up with Amen Houtep the 4th, and went to the city of 'the horizon of the sun'.*** (Akhenatons city at Amana)

Amy: Never! Surely never? ***Yes! Yes, as an elderly…… a very elderly priest.***

Amy: That's beautiful... that's... ***Right! Now I'm sorting out what you're letting me see, by the way.***

Bob: Oh? Alright. ***You're not letting me into very much I might tell you, but that's good because there are certain areas that you must rediscover for yourself. I merely give you an identification with that particular period which was a great training period, and initiation for many souls. When you realize that there's been no country on earth that has had 3000 years of unbroken spiritual training – which Egypt did, since historical times, up until your latest dispensation 2000 years ago. 3000 years of unbroken temple training of initiates, priests, and priestesses; can you imagine how many went in for initiation during those 3000 years?***

Bob: Thank you so much Johnny it is important to me, you have often spoken about the human mind getting in the way and I've always felt that I'm on the path of light but have never been certain, it's nice that a little bit of confirmation is coming through. ***Well you've always known that you were special - that you had something special to do, and that's because you planned this particular incarnation - more or less, along with others of us,***

you knew you had something special to do. Your inner self told you intuitively that much had been poured into you, and therefore much is expected from you, you've always known this. Now it's going to unfold for you most wonderfully, quietly, serenely, and powerfully. There will come to you increasingly, those who will want to know how to walk in the mud of Earth, yet feel the cool breezes of cloud nine, in their hair. People will want to know how to find balance, and you will be able to teach them how to find balance.

Bob: Now I feel maybe I have a right, before I didn't feel worthy.

Amy: He's a stooge Johnny... listen to him Johnny, squash him! squash him! ***Not if I look at the size of him, to squash him. Yes, you've always been high up in things - tall as a person too, you've always been like that. Well you will know through your humility that you will conquer everything; you know that it is humility that is your strongest point, but one doesn't have to be a well-worn doormat to consider yourself humble, gee that's got nothing to do with it, that's what is meant by abject poverty.***

Bob: Then Joan and I have been together quiet a lot before this incarnation? ***Yes... in different ways. There are many with whom you have been close to in many ways, and particularly in human relationships; when light channels meet or find an affinity in another, it's not always easy to see that the best way of working together, is through detachment. Many light channels have come to grief in personal relationships, not realizing that it was not necessary for close intimate relationships, to take place; that is the risk run by light channels, who incarnate at the same time to work together. It is important that their relationships do not become personally entangled. You may well meet others where this has taken place; they've mistaken a common affinity - well really a spiritual affinity, for personal relationships.*** (The reader will realize that Johnny is suggesting that Joan and I fell into this trap, in a previous incarnation. This was to be confirmed by an out of body past life recall that I had, which will be explained later on in this book)

Amy: Because the human emotions interfere, and it comes to grief. ***Yes the human emotions meet fire and spirit, then get bogged down in the mud.***

Bob: Thank you. ***Now your work for your land - and when I say your land I mean this whole vast area,*** (Southern Africa) ***and for the world, is blessed, and will unfold in its nice quiet almost hidden way, but it will work. The powerful work that you do in the soul is what this planet needs more than anything else at the moment, because there are an awful lot of people running around like chickens without heads.***

Bob: Thank you, Johnny. ***Right next one...Have you got a next one?***

Bob: I have one more question…… Umm every now and again I get a flash of a dream as I'm waking up; I feel that I'm working somewhere - together with others, or doing something with others, is it possible to clarify that? ***Yes very much so; your work on the inner planes, particularly now - and I talk of you as an individual and nobody else with whom you are working, is to try and heal divisions between people. You have the ability to do this, and its being done in your sleep states. There are times in your sleep state when - when you don't quite go fishing, but on a sort of 'Cooks tour', around the place to see old familiar sights and meet with familiar friends and people. You also relax on the inner planes you know? But your real work is to build bridges between people….. that is your task, and what you have dedicated yourself to, and it's what you want more than anything else. I think you realize that when people learn to live and work together in love and harmony, then the world begins to tick in the right way.***

We bless your sanctuary and this sanctuary also. You are linked, and you link with many; the great work will unfold in quietness, and will come to you. So we bless you and your families and your circumstances in all abundance, in all light, in all truth, and in all love, so be it! Blessings and greetings, beloved sisters and brothers. Johnny.

George woke up shaking slightly, then looking at me he smiled, raised a hand to his head and said, 'wow! The crackle in my ears….. it must have been Johnny'. Amy said 'Yes it was, and then. I think you must go and rest now.' George retired to his room, and Amy and I spoke for a short while before she excused herself, explaining they usually went to bed early. I sat on the veranda stunned! Me a channel of light, was I worthy enough? I knew my faults and weaknesses, and the many errors I had made in life, how could I be worthy?

It was with sadness that I said good-by to them in the morning. Amy gave me some tapes to take back - including Johnny's communication to Joan and myself on the previous evening. During the drive back to Bulawayo I replayed the tape; a five star group on earth that had been together during many past incarnations. Later on I was to learn that we were all in Palestine at the time of Jesus! Over the years I had many flashbacks about Egypt; lying in a sarcophagus of a pyramid - as an adept I think, a type of discipleship training. I also had flashbacks of sand and red/yellow sandstone cliffs on the eastern side of a beautiful River that I knew to be the Nile. Camels had not been prominent in these visions, but I do remember a secret valley going eastwards from the Nile opposite a new city that was being built which still contains hidden secrets buried under ground, that are yet to be discovered.

I had many recalls of a small temple room surrounded by vast pillars with hieroglyphs on them - an altar in Karnak, I think? I see myself checking that the servants are keeping it clean; it is a quiet sacred place but a little dark, apart from the oil lamps on the walls. There is a simple altar with fresh cut flowers, and the floor is gleaming; I sense that the alter servants are frightened of me. I live in a small room behind the sanctuary which is furnished with a table, chair, and a small reed bedding mat. There is something significant about the Altar table - a large polished slab of dark stone, something very important, but I can't remember what? The inner courtyard leads out to large hieroglyphic columns where those who wish to pray in my sanctuary, wait until the service is due to start. I have very few demands; the servants bring me food, yet I live a reclusive life. I remember that my Altar and the seating area had to be spotless.

On arriving in Bulawayo, I phoned Joan immediately arranging to visit her in the morning. We had tea during which I gave her a brief overview of what had transpired in Johannesburg. I asked her if she could remember what she had been doing around 5pm. the previous afternoon; she thought for a while then said, 'Oh yes I remember, Rod was in the workshop, supper was on the stove, so I went to lay down on the bed in the sewing room for a short while. Why do you ask?' I put the tape on and when it was finished I looked at Joan who just smiled at me, she was not over-awed like I was. On a few occasions when we'd been together on Tuesday mornings - our regular private time together, she hinted that we knew each other from a past life in Egypt, but I'd never considered it seriously. She turned to me one day and said very seriously, 'Once in Egypt you left me without saying goodbye, and I never saw you again' I pressed her for more information, but she just smiled. The world-wide Emissary of Divine Light gathering was to take place at the Gwaai hotel a year later and, it was there that Joan's statement was clarified.

Chapter 2

THE AVATAR

Bulawayo, November 1993.

I received a telephone call from Amy, during which she said; Bob we have finally been given the name of the Avatar, its Sai Baba, have you heard of him? I confessed I had only recently heard his name mentioned, but knew nothing about him. We were both excited about this long-awaited news. Amy said she would post a copy of the message to me, right away. I phoned Joan giving her the information and, like me, she couldn't wait for the tape to arrive.

Our Bulawayo gathering of light group met as usual the following Saturday morning, and we shared the news about Sai Baba, asking if anyone knew about him; Thelma thought that a spiritual friend of hers, Juan Basson, might help, and gave me his telephone number. Bulawayo had a small but strong spiritual community working on different paths to divine understanding; we respected each other's paths, and occasionally met up at holistic fairs or other people's houses. I phoned Juan saying we had some interesting news the other day, and wondered if you know anything about Sai Baba? He recalled that a Pharmacist in Bulawayo named Kiran Praji had mentioned Sai Baba, and gave me his telephone number. I phoned Kiran immediately, referring to my conversation with Juan, then went on to explain that we had just been given the name of the incarnate Avatar, and that it was Sai Baba; he responded guardedly, so I suggested we meet as soon as possible and were invited to his house that evening.

I picked up Joan and we drove to Kiran's house, where we met his wife Sudah, his children, and his father. He was slim with dark hair, and about 35 years of age, with an easy sociable personality. Sudah was quiet and open with a shy smile when she communicated. The children were about 6 and 9 years of age. They lived in their father's house because Sudah and Kiran felt he needed looking after following the death of his wife. It transpired that he was the chairman of an active group of Sai Baba devotees, in Bulawayo. I told them of Joan and my role as focalizers of the Bulawayo gathering of Light group, and about the work that we did. I asked him about his reaction to my confirmation that Sai Baba was the Avatar, asking if he was well known. Of course, he responded, He has millions of followers, and is known as the Avatar of Love.

We were told about their understanding of Swami and how Swami contacted devotees in the most unusual ways; we were also told about Vibhuuti – a manifestation of grey aromatic powder that appeared on his photographs altars or sanctuaries, a blessing or acknowledgment to the devotee that Swami knew of them, and honoured them. They brought some for us demonstrating the ceremony of putting a little on the forehead, the heart, and then the tongue. I remembered that taste and the aromatic smell of vibhuuti? It seemed to come back to us, down the corridors of time; Joan and I looked at each other and laughed in joy. We shared our early spiritual experiences with them, and it seemed that each of us had been on our own perfect paths to enlightenment. I felt a great acknowledgment of oneness with Kiran, and when we made eye contact, it was as if our eyes did the talking. The evening went too quickly and on leaving Sudah gave us books about Swami, and a recently released video-tape entitled 'God lives in India'. I arranged to contact Kiran once the Avatar tape arrived from Johannesburg.

After many years of asking who the incarnate Avatar was, and many vague references, and inferences, that he was incarnate on earth at this time, from the many beings who regularly communicated with the Arel group, they seemed reluctant to give a name, for reasons known only to them? On one occasion Amy said, beloved one, you have not yet told us the name of this Avatar**,** the entity responded; ***The time is not yet right, one day you will learn who he is.*** The much awaited tape arrived a few days later, and Kiran came to my house to listen to it; he was very impressed by the message from an entity who had been communicating with the group in Johannesburg for many years, by the name of Avon. As mentioned previously the information and reference to the Avatar was very short and matter of-a-fact, but in the months that followed, further detailed information would be forthcoming.

I gave Kiran an overview on full trance channelling, and the channel George Adams, then explained how the Arel light channel centre had begun, 24 years earlier. He asked me about Amy, who seemed to be the main questioner; I explained that Amy constantly queried what was being given during the many channelling sessions that took place. I also explained that the beings communicating insisted that the group challenge them, and ask them questions.

Amy was writing her second book at the time, based on information from the tapes, entitled **Journey beyond tomorrow,** and an earlier book called **Man the divine adventurer** had been successfully printed 10 years prior, and came about as a result of the reading of chapter, and verse, of the Aquarian gospel of Jesus the Christ. Simeon - who had been communicating regularly with the group at that time, opened the Aquarian Gospel communications. Amazingly, most of the persons mentioned in that book came through to give deeper insights into events that had unfolded in Jerusalem 2000 years earlier, and the apparent missing years of the master Jesus' life.

Eight years of asking who the incarnate Avatar was, and before that, sixteen years of discipleship training by the brotherhood of light, - the White brotherhood, and many other entities. Twenty four years to unlearn man's understanding of God, and Jesus, from the perspective of the Bible, and many other incredible beings who came to earth, and left their messages for mankind to follow.

In a communication from Avon - an ascended master known by many names from history, early information was given about the Avatar, but not his name. The following extract has been taken from a tape dated the 2/5/85; ***You are now ready from the spiritual plane to take mankind forwards into his next concept, which is man as a planetary being. Incarnating now - and perhaps Avon should not use the word incarnating for to Avon even to descend to the etheric plane is to incarnate, are many of your great leaders from your historical past on your planet. They are now preparing for earth man to step free and become one of the great galactic brother-hood. Great beings - who have been law givers down through past ages, are ready to bring about the spirit of cosmic law, which will enter into the materialistic body***

of your world community - when certain adjustments have been made, to establish forever the spiritual law of love and light.

You have a great cosmic leader with a council of twelve working with him, who have incarnated many times in certain areas of your earth throughout your history, in order to bring a new aspect of evolution to man. The, umm..... president and his board of directors, are now ready to move into world spiritual government and that time is close upon you. This time of Taurus is very important for the hierarchy of your planet - working from Shamballa, and will be the strongest period of inflow that your earth has ever known. There are more channels of light now, who are aware of the personal and corporate plan, of which they are a part. They will be the inductors of divine energy.

(Amy: Beloved one, you say a great cosmic being. May we ask you perhaps, under which name we know him by?)***He has been known under so many names in man's history. The Greek designation the *Kristos,**** (*See end of chapter) ***is the only one that can possibly be recognized, for we are talking not only of an individual but the collective soul of all man. We are talking about the sum total of the intelligence of man through his planetary and cosmic logos, or Kristos. The time of personalities will assume a new meaning for you because many have come to man in the name of the Kristos, or the Messiah. The Messiah is the ever coming one; he will not bear a designation that would set him apart from other races of man. He comes in full consciousness as the Kristos. Avon will not go into this one at this time, for another experience lies before you. Sufficient to say, that he has been ever coming, to mankind.***

The fullness of his mission to mankind came 2000 years ago in your time, (Jesus) ***representing the Creator father, or the Kristos. These are limiting terms, he who comes, comes as an individual soul, because you can only recognize the Kristos upon the inner plane of your being. Man's true brotherhood dawns now in HIS consciousness.***

Twenty four years of full trance channelled messages from hundreds of beings - many known to mankind, from history during the past 2000 years, who would take the Arel group through the inner deeper meanings of our Bible, and other religious teachings. They were encouraged to ask questions and challenge what was being given, not to blindly accept any teaching or explanation. ***Meditate on this.... think about this,*** the group were be told. ***You are our beloved brothers and sisters of light and have forgotten these truths that we give you. Your human mind has lost its link with your higher consciousness - your soul, it has shut it out and even tried to make your soul mind deny it, over many incarnations. This is why some of you have spent so much time in the lower astral planes of illusion, only to reincarnate again in disillusion'***.

The teachers continued to come through with their messages; some were Avatars, or Prophets who had incarnated on earth, or appeared to mankind, in times of great need, on the cusp of a new dispensation, when the Cherubim would hand over the keys of an old dispensation, to the Seraphim of the new age of Pisces. 2000 years later the keys would again be handed over, opening a doorway into the New Age of Aquarius in excitement, for much was to be given to mankind, which will be covered elsewhere in this book.

The Arel centre continued to receive full trance communications to re-awaken the group in the ancient wisdom teachings. The group were devout Christians, who loved Jesus very much and only knew the teachings from the Bible, so all other religions or beliefs were suspicious to them. Hadn't the Bible said, 'Beware the false prophets? The years and the teachings rolled by, and then Jesus came through, and when they realized who was talking he said; ***Please do not be in awe of me, you are not children and this is not a schoolroom and there's an absence of school marms.*** He also urged them to question him, as did all the disciples, and Archangels, pointing out that it was only by challenging or seeking clarification on what was being given, that their understanding and spiritual growth on the ancient wisdom teachings, could be measured.

Aureal (Uriel) - one of the Archangel's, gave this beautiful insight to the group. It was channelled on the 7/10/83; ***We invite you - if you get the opportunity,*** (divine humour) ***to ask your questions. Please question a little - because as we have said before, when***

you formulate your questions with your human mind, we are able to judge the decree to which we can communicate with you. We do not wish to embarrass you in any way either by not giving you sufficient material, where-with to initiate discussions, or perhaps by giving you too much, which you might be unfamiliar with.

Once again Aureal will apologize for perhaps covering old ground. It is to enable us to become more familiar with the territory that you are more familiar with, that we do so. You are at a stage where you are re-grasping your former state of being, and consciousness, but which for you is strange. Your consciousness has been cut off from its awareness of its source, it has become embedded in a basic low life vibration, so you have to work yourself up through the various levels of your consciousness, to recapture the truth of your being. Do you wish to speak? ..... you do not have to, Aureal is not putting pressure on you; if you are following me, then there is no need to ask questions, but you must interrupt if you wish.

And then the time was right to tell the group, that the **COSMIC CHRIST** was, **BHAGAVAN SRI SATHYA SAI BABA** - the ever coming one, the Lord God of hosts, the Avatar of synthesis, and the father who sent Jesus to earth. 'SWAMI' - an affectionate name given to Sai Baba by his devotees, was 67 years of age at the time we were given his name, and the question should be asked why none of us knew of him, when millions of western and eastern devotees and disciples did. Possibly we were all so wrapped up in our own paths that we did not have the need to look further a-field; strangely, his name had been mentioned to me shortly before Amy phoned, nothing happens by chance!

An incredible entity from the Old Testament using an Egyptian name – **RA AB HOUTEP**, gave this information, in a communication dated the 6/10/94; ***When god fills the whole room of your mind, then your only desire is to become one with him. There will come a time when it will click in you, and you will be ready to move out of the restricting life, in matter worlds. This is the importance of the age you are living in now..... that is the importance of the incarnate Avatar. Your aspirations have drawn*** *down a great consciousness who adopted a form that you now know, the form of man, but it is only a form.*

You are living in unique times because the all consciousness -living in the world of man, is able to affect every level of creation on the planet including the kingdoms; this incarnation is a result of the aspirations of many souls over the last century, to become omniscient, omnipresent, and omnipotent, which is the goal of the gods achieved.

JOHNNY – 28/7/95; *It does not matter to the Avatar, or great spiritual leaders, what people think, believe, or say about them; do what you can to exemplify in your life, what those great ones did in their lives. Don't be too concerned about the violent attacks being made, on beloved Jesus, he knows how to handle that lot. Sometimes it's more difficult to handle his admirers, but that's up to them. Become detached from your own personal point of view no matter how right you may feel they are, wherever you can, emanate that power of love, and light, unconditionally. Your Swami is the reference point incarnate, for anyone reaching their god self within, that's why he incarnated. The great divine incarnates anytime when the darkness seems to be getting the upper hand. In this moment let's attune with Swami Sathya Sai Baba. Consciously attune now, and be aware of the presence of incarnate divinity, what a wonderful thrill it is for all concerned, either on the physical, or inner planes. Know that He is the answer to the prayer that has gone out, for centuries of time.*

DWALL KHUUL -16/11/95; *You enter a consciousness experience now that will take you through to a resurrected period, the like of which the earth has not yet witnessed; in the words of your great one who trod the path of man and opened up heaven itself, 'lo I am with your always'. Your planet is awakening now in an incredible burst of glory and brotherhood.... all the star houses of great Galactica are channelling through the great wheel of light. Focus upon your heart centre, and the great ashram centre in Southern India. You may intone your prayer, which will change your world in*

the twinkling of an eye.(The Great Invocation was en-toned three times)

RA AB HOUTEP - 29/9/94; ***The great incarnate Avatar has come into the world experience at this time, to be a focal point for those who desire to serve. Service is the great sign of Libra; do not look for results of your actions, just be willing to serve and to give. Do what you know is the right thing to do, difficult as it always is. Now is an excellent time to be initiated into the higher orders of service. Service is the great key to this particular sign, and the energy of the descending Christ light and angelic kingdoms. This is a wonderful time, . . you have been touched on the shoulder, to work with a great incarnate Avatar.***

(Amy: Beloved one the Avatars Elephant Sai Gita, that cries when he's not there; it has such a close bond with him and he uses that love to show people that love is bringing the Elephant up to human consciousness.) ***Yes indeed that is so, you are the ones who are preparing the way for the reappearance of the Avatar, you are working now consciously, with the Avatar soul group. Your identification and love, with your brothers and sisters on this path, is to focalize the intention of the incarnate Avatar, who is lifting up the whole of the race of the world, and the kingdoms.***

Feel at all times included in the great Avatar love, feel the presence within you, and around you, it is this that the Avatar - Sai Baba, is attempting to get across to his devotees, and everyone, to serve with no strings attached. This is why he does not wave his magic wand and lift poverty out of the land, because a soul in that situation has got to realize its own Karma, and true nature. As a result of the incarnation of this Avatar, and the previous one, and the one before, many have reached their last incarnation in human form.

Kiran was invited to join our Saturday morning meditation meetings with the rest of our group, which he accepted when his work commitments allowed. The vibes between us were good - love and animated sharing the order of the day; he resonated very strongly with the Arel messages, and we learned more about Swami from him. We learnt about the Hindu lesser gods, and the devotee's greeting as a way of acknowledging Swami, Om Sai Ram. We were given many exciting insights about Swami's work on earth and first hand experiences that the Bulawayo devotees had witnessed, whilst visiting Puttaparthi - Swami's ashram in Southern India. Many had personal experiences of his manifestations of Vibhuuti, trinkets or rings at Dharshan - an opportunity every morning to be in his presence and energy, and hopefully receive a personal blessing, or invitation to an interview with him.

We learnt that Swami would accept or reject hand-held letters for him, because he knew the contents, or the karma, involved before even touching them. Because an Avatar is Omniscient, (all knowing) Swami would sometimes completely ignore the pleadings of a mother for her deformed child; this would seem strange to the western mind, but did not Jesus speak of sowing and reaping? KARMA - suffering in the physical realm, is tied-in with the soul's actions in past incarnations, and Swami will not interfere with a person's Karma - indeed he has no right to, except where his divine intervention is for the greater good of humanity. In relation to a person pleading to Swami for help for a suffering child - or whatever, Swami sees the past Karma immediately and knows that it might or should play out as suffering in a present incarnation. Swami knows that for us to reach our godhead we must reap what we have sown.

We attended some of the Hindu ceremonies, where we met and bonded with a lot of the devotees, who would eventually become our friends. We learnt of their understanding and love for Swami, and they in turn gained a deeper awareness of Swami, and spirituality, when they listened to our tapes.

We watched the video that Sudah had leant us, during our regular Saturday morning gathering; two in the group resonated with it, but others were uncertain. Coming from a fundamental Christian background and with western concepts and culture, it is not easy to suddenly except the truth in other religions. Hinduism is a philosophy not a religion and it seemed that the discipleship training that the Johannesburg group had gone through over many years, would needs-be necessary for some of our group. Amy and others in the Johannesburg group never ceased to seek clarification on all manner of things concerning Sai Baba, so when these tapes arrived we shared them with the Sai group, to add further clarification about the Avatar of love.

The relationship between us was almost an enigma to other Sai Baba groups, in Southern Africa; sadly throughout history people of different ethnic race or religious persuasions had kept themselves apart, seeing themselves as different from each other. This often leads towards tribal, clan, or national separation, but this was just not the case in Bulawayo. Swami would show Zimbabwe that the Avatar's message of unconditional love was manifest.

It was about 4 months since we had learnt about Swami, and many of the younger devotees were now attending our Saturday morning, or Thursday evening, attunements whilst some of our group were joining in with their sacred gatherings or honouring. I leant Kiran the tape of Johnny's communication to Joan and myself; a few days later he phoned saying he would call in after work to return it. We discussed Johnny's communication to Joan and myself, and after tea he told me the story of how Swami had come into his life, a truly amazing story.

Bob I was a total waster for many years of my life. I was a qualified Pharmacist, earning good money, married with a lovely wife and children, but I drank too much. I was always the fun and life of every party, and no sooner had work finished then I would go to the club for a drink, getting home around 7.30, often very tipsy or plain drunk. Unfortunately - or should I say fortunately, I had a serious heart problem and was taking about 20 tablets a day, but despite this, I continued to drink too much. One evening, I was sitting at the bar laughing and enjoying myself, when I collapsed; an ambulance was called, and I was rushed into emergency. I was to learn later that my heart had stopped beating twice in the Ambulance, and that in the emergency room my heart stopped beating again. Resuscitation was attempted by shock treatment, there-after my heart would start beating again but eventually it just stopped! They gave up on me, but after about 9 minutes it started beating normally again. I spent two weeks in hospital and was eventually released for home recuperation, and rest.

About two weeks later I was sitting on my mother's bed, she hadn't been very well, I held her hand as she slept; suddenly a small very bright light appeared on my left near the door, about 4 feet above the ground. I looked at it in astonishment as it grew bigger, then I shook my mother's hand to awaken her. A being of light was manifesting before my eyes; it slowly became physical, and I became frightened. I shook my mother's hand, Mom wake up….. wake up! Then the entity said to me, 'She will not wake up' I said to this person, 'who are you what do you want with me' but he just smiled lovingly at me, which made me feel calmer.

He was a small man with very fuzzy hair - he looked like an American rock star, and was wearing a traditional Hindu dhoti. **He** smiled again saying; ***'do not be fearful, have you forgotten me so soon…… and the promise you made to me?'*** I was confused and uncertain, and said, what promise, what promise? He smiled at me with such compassion, and then I became aware of an incredible eminence of love, and wisdom; then he said, ***I will remind you of your promise. Four weeks ago you died in the emergency ward of the Hospital…… as you were dying you called out to God, begging and pleading for your life, so I came to you and we talked. I asked you, do you really want to live, and you said yes, I don't want to die. I told you I could give you your life back, but that you would have to work for me, in my name. You agreed and promised me that you would open a centre in my name; I told you at the time you were dying, and I will tell you again, I AM SATHYA SAI BABA.***

Bob, I knew that what he told me was the truth, it was a deep inner knowing. He told me to hold out my hand palm upwards, then he raised his hand above it in a circular motion a few times, and my hand overflowed with grey aromatic powder that he told me was Vibhuuti. He said it was a blessing he was offering me, and that I should take a pinch of this in a small glass of water in the morning, and evening; he continued, ***throw away all your tablets, you will never need them again.***

He smiled at me again - love permeating the whole room, and then slowly dematerialized, and was gone! My mother woke up immediately he had left….. I tried to explain what had happened, but she didn't believe me; then I showed her the Vibhuuti. She looked at me long and searchingly, then got up and brought me an empty medicine jar to put it in. She asked me more questions about what had happened, but I was still trying to come to terms with it. My life has changed forever since that day, and I have never taken tablets again……. I have been to see him in India on two occasions since that day, and we are planning another visit with some devotees this year.

Kiran Pradji formed the official Sai Baba organization in Bulawayo, and it soon grew into a disciplined, service orientated organization. From our tapes we had learnt that an Avatar is; OMNIPRESENT - everywhere at the same time, OMNISCIENT - all knowing, and OMNIPOTENT - eternal, immortal, and indestructible, yet incarnate as a human being. Within his omniscience, certain events were to occur in Zimbabwe concerning the continuing expansion of love and service to that country; we learnt that two of his devotees from Denmark would be coming to Bulawayo to open an orphanage - in service to him and that a strong centre of love and light, would issue forth from that area of Southern Africa.

A month before Swami's birthday, a 24 hour devotional honouring was to take place at Vas and Bharti Patel's house in honour of Shiva and other Hindu gods and goddesses. A beautiful shrine was set up featuring a picture of Shiva and statues of Swami and Sai Baba of Shirdi - Swami's last incarnation. It was decorated with beautiful flowers, plants, and silk drapes. Our group was invited to participate for two one hour sessions. Joan and I attended the 1a.m. to 2a.m.honouring and Wendy Staples joined us in the morning session. Bhajans - Hindu holy songs and mantras were sung and prayers were given; in-between times, meditations took place continually over the 24 hour period ending on the Saturday evening at 6.00 p.m.

Just after 11 am on Sunday morning, the phone rang. It was Kiran, who summarily 'ordered' me to be at the gate in five minutes; he actually said, 'Bob I'm coming to pick you up right now, be at the gate, I want to show you something amazing'. I had never heard Kiran so animated, so obviously something very important had happened. I had barely put my shoes on when he hooted at the gate. We drove off in the direction of Vas and Bharti's house; on arrival we found a lot of cars parked outside, and many visitors moving in and out of the house, including a few Sai Baba devotees. I assumed we were helping to pack up the altar, but Kiran whisked me off to Vas and Bharti's spare bedroom. Unbeknown to me, it was a permanent sanctuary to Swami, and other Hindu gods. As we walked into the room a strong aroma of Vibhuuti was evident, then Kiran pointed to the Altar table in the corner. Everything was covered in vibhuuti, all the ornaments on it, a Christian cross, the table surface, and a large dressing mirror.

Kiran said, 'Bob, look at this'. In front of the altar was a perfect AUM symbol, in yellow vibhuuti; about 3 inches in diameter? The Hindu Ohm symbol, is similar to the number 30 written in script. We stood quietly together amazed. We looked at each other and then as if on cue, we both shivered involuntary; Kiran whispered, 'Bob, he's here now.' I said, Yes, Kiran, he is. We hugged each other in joy. Standing together with his arm around my shoulder, we were oblivious to others of the Hindu community, until Vimal walked in, and we all hugged. Some of the Hindu community came in and out of the room leaving money on the Alter, which I must confess, upset me a little. Many devotees came and went, some kneeling on the floor, or prostrating themselves, in front of a small statue of Swami. The room was a hive of activity; some were placing photographs of Swami on the floor, or on whatever space was available on the Alter, which was rapidly becoming congested. This was to be the first shrine that Swami would bless with his presence, in Bulawayo; others were to follow.

Kiran dropped me off and I phoned Joan immediately telling her what had happened and arranging to pick her up around 4.30 to take her to Vas and Bharti's house. In the car Joan told me she had phoned the rest of the group, giving them the news of the manifestation. We walked into the house and were greeted by a few of the younger devotees who knew us from our Saturday, and Thursday, gatherings; we hugged us in excitement, whilst some of the traditional Hindus, stared at us in surprise. The Bulawayo Hindu community, were to learn a lot, in the unfolding years, about Swami's message of unconditional love, and the relationship between our two groups.

Vibhuuti was starting to form throughout the room; on family photographs, and all the new pictures, and ornament, that had been placed on the altar that morning. We picked up Wendy the next day and took her to the shrine; the yellow OHM sign was even more prominent, standing out amongst the grey Vibhuuti. Kiran explained to me, that the area that Shiva came from was well known for its yellow clay like soil. (Shiva is god of the holy Hindu trinity, the other two being Brahma and Vishnu).

As usual, I preferred to visit the shrine when others were not there, and about four days after the manifestation had begun, I called in again. I was particularly drawn to an elongated photograph of Swami, in a white silk gown, that someone had placed against the floor of the shrine; I bent down to get a closer look at him and said quietly to myself 'Swami you are beautiful'….. and then the photograph fell slowly forwards into my hands. I shivered, then laughingly put it back against the altar wall and said, thank you Swami. Vibhuuti had continued to manifest over everything including a large new photograph of Mary, with Jesus super-imposed in her heart, which had recently been hung on the wall, to the left of the altar.

I had grown to love Swami deeply, and more so because of the deeper information we continued to get on the tapes, concerning his vast cosmic being-ness. This divine incarnation is no mere prophet, or guru, he is THE COSMIC CHRIST, LOVE INCARNATE - AND THE FATHER WHO SENT JESUS TO EARTH. We were to learn in the coming months that the world is yet to really understand his magnificence, and of special joy to me, was that I was being given signs that he acknowledged me. I visited the shrine regularly, usually during working hours when no one else was there. On one such visit I noticed that the curtain and part of the altar had caught alight; I was to learn from Vas that the wind had blown the lace curtain onto the oil lamp when no-one was home, and that the table, and pelmet had burnt, yet the photograph of Swami, was untouched!

Amy and George were kept informed about all of these events, and our activities with the Sai group. They had tried to make contact with the Sai Baba community in Johannesburg, but found them very difficult to communicate with, and suspicious, of non-Hindus. I sent them a photograph of Swami that I had placed on the altar, and which had been blessed by Him with Vibhuuti; unfortunately during its framing much was lost, but I believe it hangs in pride of place in their sanctuary, and know that they were thrilled to get it.

Kiran related another amazing story to me that occurred whilst he was on a visit to Puttapharti. He went with a few of the Bulawayo Sai group, for an important Hindu festival; there were thousands of adherents trying to get access to Swami's morning Dharshan, so a ticket system had been introduced whereby numbered tickets, would allow access to specific seating lines. Unfortunately there was not enough room outside Swami's house to allow everyone to attend Dharshan. The entry tickets were drawn from a box, and the lucky ones, with a numbered ticket, were allocated a seat in one of the many lines. This was considered to be the fairest way of giving all his devotees an equal chance, of attending his morning blessings.

Sometimes one of Swami's staff would arrive unannounced at your door, to let you know that Swami wished to see you at a certain time; this had happened to Kiran on other occasions, and was a special honouring that only a few devotees were blessed to have, when visiting his ashram. On this visit, he was neither invited to an interview, or able to get a numbered access ticket. Swami has incredible demands on his time with delegations visiting him from all over the world; it seemed that the Bulawayo group had chosen a busy time to visit him. About a week before Kiran was due to return to Zimbabwe, he managed to get a seat at Dharshan and related the following story to me.

I had a seat far away from Swami's normal Dharshan route. I was wearing the yellow neck scarf of a youth helper, so I was officially on duty. Swami came near our line, but was still about 50 ft in front of me, I really hoped that he would see me, or look at me, but he didn't. A man in front of me was having extreme problems with 'Puttapharthi tummy', so I had to help him back to his room. By the time I got back to Dharshan, Swami was just entering his house; disappointed I bent down to pick up my blanket and discovered that there was a sweet on it? The man next to me saidSwami turned away from his usual Dharshan route, and then he manifested the sweet, and told me to tell you it was he who put the sweet on your blanket.

Omniscience! One day the world will really understand what that means, because that level of divine consciousness is within our grasp!

Jesus entered into his full Avatar-ship at his baptism in the Jordan, and thereafter he began his mission in earnest; did he not manifest bread, and fish, to feed hundreds of his followers, and did he not appear and disappear at will? Sometimes Swami could be very exasperating to those that wanted to see him, or just be near him; his Omniscience sometimes chose the timing for lessons in humility. He teaches his followers that first they should learn to control their egos, and once done, his summoning of them would be perfect. There are many books on the market about this incredible incarnation, and I would recommend the reader to seek them out; one that is particularly important for the western minded person is entitled 'The Psychiatrist and the Guru'.

I use the word incarnate with much significance, for an Avatar does not need to incarnate through woman; an Avatar has total control over all aspects of the physical and spiritual universe, therefore being capable of forming a human body by thought and intention, the modern terminology is transmutation. Swami chose to incarnate through woman at incredible sacrifice, to show us that we too, are God! He once told a congregation '***The difference between you and me is that I know I'm god, you only think you might be; in reality there is no difference between us, only our conscious awareness of who we truly are'.***

Avatars are of the ascended master group, also known as the sons of god. Jesus the Christ came to earth as an Avatar, but because he incarnated through the blessed Mary, he only reconnected with that high state of being-ness, after he received the full Christ light at his baptism in the Jordan. He knew that his mission was to come to earth as the son of man, yet also the son of god; as a high initiate he also made the sacrifice of a physical incarnation, to show us that ***'Things that I do you can do, and even greater things'.*** He was called the only begotten son of god, because he was born into the world through woman. The symbology of his death on the cross was just that - symbology, he transmuted his body from form into light, appearing or disappearing at will, after his resurrection, as an Avatar.

Resurrection, Ascension, transcendence and trans-mutation are different levels of the same cosmic principle, - AS ABOVE SO BELOW, and in relation to the future of mankind as ascended beings,

AS BELOW SO ABOVE, because all form will return to source, sooner than mankind realizes. As ascended beings, our quantum leap into cosmic consciousness is not very far away, and that is why BHAGAVAN SRI SATHYA SAI BABA IS HERE.

Prior to this book going into print, Swami left his earth body on the 17th of April, 2011. This does not change anything in this chapter, or other chapters, on the Avatar, within this book. The messages of The Buddha, and the Christ - Jesus, are as vital today as they were when they were first given, thousand s of years ago. Swami has always said, ***'My real work is on the inner planes of consciousness'*** and ever has this been the message of all great teachers, that have come to earth. Some of his devotees are devastated and surprised that he 'died', but this is far from the truth.

I believe that all negative earth Karma - up until his departure, is now safely contained within his physical body; it was necessary for him to 'die' for mankind, just as Jesus did! As an Avatar, Swami could have transmuted his body into light, and continue with his physical earth mission, but now he is able to fulfil his planetary mission to earth, the kingdoms, and the whole of humanity. Many years ago Swami said he would leave earth in 2011; it seems to me that he made the transition sooner, because of humanities raised consciousness, NOW HIS REAL WORK WILL BEGIN!

(* The Kristos is a Greek word meaning 'light'. Translations from Aramaic and Latin to English brought about the word Christ. - See Mathew 16)

Chapter 3

G O D

Let there be light and creation.

The channel centre in Johannesburg started receiving full-trance channelled messages in the late 60s, and since that time to date, over 4500 communications have come through from divine mind, on the ancient wisdom or mystery teachings. All communications were recorded on audio tapes. Many teachings about light, creation, the atom, the experiment of earth, the spiritual etheric and soul realms, and the manifest realms of creation, were given on a question and answer basis. These diverse subjects were explained to the group in incredible detail; deep insights from Jesus, the disciples, Archangels, the Brotherhood of Light - also known as the White Brotherhood, the sons and daughters of god, and many other entities, who had incarnated during the past 35,000 years. Some of them are known to mankind from history, and gave fascinating insight, and perspectives, about let there be light, from a spiritual standpoint.

I humbly offer some of these teachings as a starting point in trying to understand let there be light and creation. It was explained to the Arel group, that they would receive the most in-depth teachings on the ancient wisdom/mystery truths, ever presented to mankind. Because of my link with the group, I am blessed to be in possession of 350 tapes, containing over 600 messages. I offer the reader simple insights, into the deeper mysteries of let there be light, and creation; mysteries only because the human mind has forgotten these truths, and we rarely have the ability to recall them.

Throughout this book I might revert to the word 'GOD' as a means of trying to put an unfathomable entity into a slot. Some readers would have sensed a long time ago, that God is not a single entity with a long white beard, sitting on a throne, somewhere above earth, in a place called heaven. Heaven - as mentioned by Jesus and other divine being's, is merely a reference point that seeks to explain that god is an omnipresent, or universal consciousness, not a specific spiritual entity.

The Tibetian master DWAAL KHUUL gave a series of short daily discourses, between the 12th, and 19th, of June 1975. This is part of one communication, explaining god; ***Blessings and greetings, beloved companions....Dwaal Khuul talks to many channels at this time. Let us remember that earth is part of a process of evolution, going through many stages, until it fulfils its purpose, which is to manifest pure light, in the cosmos of all being. There is a creator of earth, and a creator - or god, of all earths, all planets, all substances, and all beings, When one understands this, one sees that god in reality is not individual. There are many creators who manifest themselves within god, therefore let us say, there are many gods. In so far as earth is concerned, the powers of creation have been delegated by HE who first of all manifested himself within the great body of darkness, as light. As he manifested himself in the great void of darkness, so did light come to be; the earth is the outer manifestation of the body of this god, therefore all that it contains and all which it is, is god, every atom of being.***

KARRATA gave this explanation about God, on the 16/8/86;***In the beginning was one light, which was love. Love envisaged another aspect of itself, which was wisdom. Love and wisdom, equated to the male/female polarity, but it was still one light. They envisaged a unity between them, and a third light formed within the one light, this light was God. This was the first triune principal, which equated to Father/Mother God, and son.***

RA NA TA - who could be described as the CEO of Shamballa, gave this explanation in trying to understand God; ***This vast intelligence could be called, The primordial initiating causal mind of everything that was, is and will be.*** God in the spiritual, etheric and soul realms is androgynous - of no specific sex, but incorporates the male/female polarity as love and wisdom. It is given that the Supreme creator created the five pointed star man/woman in his image and likeness - that being the case, God/Goddess would be a more correct designation. The ***ELOHIM*** - the creator lords of light, formulated the plan of light in the beginning, before the word was spoken.

There are many other aspects of 'God' in relation to the spiritual realms - the Kristos which equates to the holy breath or **PRANA**(Channelled information below), the Spirit and Soul, the etheric atom, Angels, the Elohim, Archangels, etc. Other aspects are our***SHAKINAH*** light body which incorporates our ***MERKABAH VEHICLE*.** The Merkabah is described as a sacred geometric pattern in the form of a dodecahedron, enabling us to move and have our being-ness anywhere in the Universes, by thought and intention. *KOLOB* is known as the centre where the will of god is known, it is also referred to as the great central sun.

The following definition of Prana was given by father SIMEON, the Sanhedrin priest who held and acknowledged the baby Jesus as the Messiah. This communication came through on the 7/4/78; ***Simeon has come out of retirement. Let us be more aware of the powers which man wields - especially when he gives his attention to them. The giving of attention to anything is the secret of dealing with it; the secret of using cosmic power is to give your attention to it, but it is like the light bulb that hangs - it merely hangs, until someone presses a switch, which puts on the light, but let us deal with the holy breath, Prana.***

(Yes, this is fabulous) ***Yes it is indeed. The mere act of breathing does not mean that you are drawing in Prana, it is much finer than the breath that you breathe - infinitely finer, it is the holy-spirit, it is God. When you give your attention to the Pranic force entering into your being through your breath, you are drawing-in God.***

(Amy; So the yogic exercises that they give, is this because they knew the secrets too?) ***When man in his consciousness, concentrates upon breathing - and Simeon uses this word breathing loosely, the absorption of Pranic force, then it is not necessary for the human body to have anything else to sustain it. It was because of Prana that man lived to such advanced years; how else shall man - even using a physical form, be an immortal and eternal being, except that he live in the concentrated awareness of breathing-in, God, Prana. The***

mighty I AM presence is of course the holy breath, or Prana if you wish God

(Amy; Is this what Jesus demonstrated, during the 40 days in the wilderness?) ***Yes! He referred to it when he said, if thine eye be single, then shall thy body be full of light. Concentrate upon the light - Prana, and your body will become filled with it. . . . I am the light of the world, think of Prana as light. The holy breath is light, and knowing this, you will read your Bible with new eyes, and new understanding. Let us attune to the cosmic light force, the holy breath, the Holy Spirit, Prana, God, or what you will. Blessings and greetings, beloved channel..... beloved friends.***

Modern terms for Prana are; the quantum hologram, the mind of god, Chi, universal energy, intelligent design, dark power/energy, electro-magnetism, etc.

I would ask the reader to bear with me, as I take them on a journey of remembrance, leading up to Let there be Light, the formation of the universes, and then the formation of our earth 5 billion years ago. Millions of years later, the new earth would be seeded by divine mind, and thereafter - thousands of years later, we would en-soul the physical forms, and bring god consciousness into creation. Our em-bodyments would involve raising the consciousness of ape/man, by en-souling them. This was to be done in harmony, love, free will, and non-violence. I apologize in advance to the spiritual hierarchy, in striving to give a simple overview to such a vast Cosmic event, but seek only to bring a little more clarity, and understanding, using simple English language.

LET THERE BE LIGHT

In the beginning was a void, and darkness filled the void, but there was movement in the darkness - a consciousness without form, YOU, and ME, and countless others. We were conscious being-ness, but without a light body; We could not see each other as we moved together in the voids, but were drawn to each other in groups of compatible vibration and energy, that we felt familiar with.

There was much love between the groups, as we communicated by thought, but not so the elemental groups, who were un-conscious, but seemed to have group leaders who would later become known as the Devic lords (the lords of all the manifest physical forms in creation) The Devic lords work with the nature spirits - or elementals, which are ever present in all creation such as; animals, trees, flowers, etc.) The elemental groups were ever present in the voids, and held the potential for physical creation of thought form when the time was right. Somehow we knew of light, desiring to have bodies of light, and to be able to see each other. There were countless groups moving throughout the voids, some of a lower vibration, and some very high.

We came across other groups that vibrated at similar levels to ours, we would discuss our yearnings for light with them; one group moving restlessly throughout the voids, would meet and talk to us. This small group comprised seven entities that were different from the rest of us, because their vibrations and energy, was incredibly high. Somehow they knew of the desire of all the groups, for light in the darkness. They told us that they were being impressed by an initiating causal mind, from an unknown source, towards a plan involving all of us; they stressed that all the groups must be part of the plan for it to be successful, even the elemental groups, They explained that this plan could not work without the elementals, because these entities had the power to bring about physical creation, from thought We were intrigued, but did not fully understand what they were telling us. We continued moving throughout the voids, meeting up with other groups; we told them that a plan towards the desire for light was being formulated.

Time passed - even though there was no time in the voids, and then a small bright light was seen. We moved towards it at the speed of thought. Seven circles had formed - one inside the other, and at the centre, a pure white light was pulsating. We watched in amazement as each of the seven high vibrational beings merged their consciousness within the light; as they did this, the light grew brighter and larger. We saw that each one of them had a body of light which comprised millions of golden white etheric stars. We were later to understand that these were etheric atoms. (Etheric atoms, entities, and worlds, are invisible to human eyes). The etheric realm is a lower vibrational energy of the pure spiritual realm, and a link between spiritual and physical creation. With-in the light we could see the seven entities individually, yet mysteriously they were ONE? They addressed us explaining what had unfolded, but we could not fully comprehend what they were saying. This event occurred over billions of years - as man understands time.

It was explained to us that first one circle was formed, and then the others; each circle moved in opposite directions to the next one, by thought and intention, the resultant reactions between these circles created swirling energy fields - a spiritual energy vortex. After the last circle formed, a pure white light blazed at its centre. This light would become known as THE ACT OF FIRST CAUSE. Divine mind explanations about the Atom, in relation to God, and light, are explained as follows;

ANDREW - **the disciple*****; The smallest grain of dust has seven bodies, which are comprised of; physical, etheric, astral, emotional, mental, soul, and a spiritual body. The electron is more minute than the atom, and has seven bodies; each body is a universe on its own, a resonation of sound, and colour, which surrounds the electron. Protons, and neutrons buzz around an electron therefore the electron is the heart of an atom. The atom is a world unto itself. A physical atom in a grain of sand is light energy, vibrating at a lower level.***

ORIEL - 27/10/83;***The atom is a spark of light and colour - an individual consciousness, nurtured by the all-light from *KOLOB* which is Prana. The atom and your solar system are identical, one is the microcosm, the other the macrocosm. You are a conscious atom..... you might say your heart and head chakras, are protons and electrons, and the lower chakras are neutron's. You are a sphere; your heart is the sun, and the atoms of your body are the planets. Neutron's, are the receivers and conductors, of energy, from your solar system. Splitting the atom creates solar energy, but it is not necessary for man to split the atom, to have solar energy. The ray energy in each atom, can be separated and used - much as your laser beam is today without violence, to produce the energy that man desires. In splitting the atom, man merely made smaller atoms. The***

smallest atom in the physical solar system is linked as one, with all atoms in the solar system.

TAUUNG (known to humanity as Archangel Gabriel)***Between the electron, and nucleus, is electro magnetism. The I AM presence penetrates every cell, atom, and photon, of creation. Everything physical is a pulsating field of energy, an etheric atom.***

We looked in awe at the circles, and saw that all were illuminated by this light. The outer circle was a deep maroon/red, the next circle was orange, then yellow, green, blue, violet, and at the centre a pure white light. IN THE BEGINNING WAS THE WORD AND THE WORD WAS WITH GOD, AND THE WORD WAS GOD**. GOD IS LIGHT!**

After each of the seven beings immersed their consciousness in the light, we were called on to do likewise; as we merged with the light, we looked at each other in wonderment, for now we too had bodies of light. After billions of years of wondering in the darkness, we could now identify each other. Each of us had our own unique colour variation, and pattern - distinguishing our light body from others of our group, and yet we were one. The groups in the outermost reaches of the voids moved towards us at the speed of thought, and we welcomed them to become one with us. The first SPIRITUAL sun of KOLOB expanded and the voids were pushed outwards, until the last of the groups merged with us. We were a cell, within the one light of Kolob.

TAUUNG - the lord of Virgo, was one of the first of the brotherhood of light to come to our galaxy and solar system, at the beginning of the experiment of Earth. This communication came through on the3/3/1984; ***Greetings and blessings, it is Tauung. We will go back in time. Picture yourselves living in a time before your Earth was seeded, and colonized. Before you is utter darkness, and yet, there is movement in the darkness; there appeared a massive star that exploded - which was its physical manifestation, and let there be light occurred. Yes the great star exploded - the big bang, and the void was no longer a void, it was light. That great star already existed in the void, but your human eyes would not have seen it – it was etheric, Spiritual.***

Indeed human eyes would not have seen the first great spiritual sun of Kolob, because this event was in the etheric spiritual realm, and the physical manifest realms, were yet to evolve. The Elohim explained to us that we would become universes, and galaxies, yet would always be one with them, and the supreme creator. We would infuse the voids as co-creators, for we were in truth, creator gods.

A sound reverberated throughout the voids...... AHH..... UU....... MM..... A harmonizing sound bringing great joy and a feeling of peace to all of us. It was the sound of our Sun, the music of KOLOB. We invited the Devic lords, and the elemental groups, to become one with us, and as they did, a transformation took place; the spiritual atoms of our light bodies, transmuted into etheric/physical atoms. And Kolob became a vast physical sun.

The seven wise one's who created the first etheric atom, would become known as the ELOHIM - the creator lords of light. We/Kolob, were now a vast physical sun, and being unable to contain our immense energy and vibration, an incredible implosion occurred - a Super Nova. We tumbled joyously into the voids, the manifest physical formation of the universes, had begun. LET THERE BE LIGHT would have been seen by human eyes; indeed human ears, would have heard the big bang. The void left over from this event, would be known as **'The centre where the will of god is known' -** as given by Dwaal Khuul, in the great invocation.

AREL gave this explanation to the group in, 1988; ***Seven Suns flew off from the first great central Sun, and from these eight suns, the manifest universes were formed. Thereafter, twelve universes were formed from each Sun. 'The centre where the will of god is known'- as given by Dwaal Khuul in his great invocation, is the great central sun of Kolob; the etheric centre from which creation began, comprising twelve etheric universes.***

JOHNNY gave this insight, during a communication dated the 6/7/78; ***Let's say god is a being; a being so far advanced, that it was given the opportunity of expressing itself into the voids of non being. This tremendous being - with the aspirations of love, desired to express itself. It exploded itself into the void, and look what happened.***

Our sun moved across the voids, and it seemed that we had barely reached the end of our journey when it, 'WE', imploded into twelve suns. In a final Super Nova, our sun tumbled into the voids, to become a universe. Our universe comprised thousands of galaxies with their suns, planets, and gas-fields, that would form new star systems, when a new impulse of let there be light was ordained, by the supreme creator. **WE WERE THE GALAXIES, THE STARS, AND THE PLANETS.** (Daniel 12, verse 3 - The star that you are)

We were to learn that a tiny star seed of our Shakinah and Merkabah body, would be used to form a sheath body, that would become known as the SOUL. Our Soul sheath body would be of a lower vibration, and energy that would not harm the physical worlds of creation, once the experiment began. Our Shakinah, Merkabah, and soul body, would become known as our, I AM PRESENCE.

SIMEON was to give the group many teachings, about the I AM presence. Herewith one of them dated the 23/6/77; ***Let us discuss the presence of life within us - and all things, the great I AM PRESENCE. Simeon would like you to ask your questions. Let us begin by saying that, he I am presence is the being of all life, and all things. It is the consciousness at the heart of all creation, be it a grain of sand, or a universe. I Am is the consciousness which is aware of self in man, who is an aware being. This consciousness devolves upon the awareness...... I. In feeling the I, you realize that you ARE, so therefore you say to yourself I AM. When you express the awareness of being, you say I AM.***

I AM is the life force which is ever seeking to manifest itself in perfection; it is in all things, and all life, it is the open door to all creation. It is that which enters into a blade of grass, a seed, the flower, the insect, animal, man, and everything. According to the awareness of our I Am in manifestation, so does the power get drawn towards it to produce a grain of sand, man himself, or a Universe. Do you understand are you quite clear?

The I am, is the ever present life force whose one purpose is to create itself. In man alone does it become a malleable, pliable substance. The life force itself is unconcerned with how it manifests, it is man alone, who can manipulate this life force consciously through his aware presence of his being, by saying,

I AM. Every time you say I AM, you create. (A few Bible references on the I Am presence can be found in; Psalm 82 verse 1 - John 10 verses 30, 34, 35, 38. - John 14 verse 10 - Acts 17 verses 27 to 29.)

Divine mind has told us that our earth is in the outer planes of creation, and that the inner planes are the spiritual/mental realms. There are 96 manifest universes, and 12 un-manifest, totalling 108. It may interest the reader to know that Buddhists, and Hindus, have 108 beads on their Japamala prayer rosary; these beads partly relate to the names, or aspects of god, and the many mansions in the fathers house. The experiment of earth would be undertaken by us, as **SOUL ENTITIES,** but only by our choice, and agreement. Initially we agreed to overshadow and en-soul the evolving ape-man, and man-ape species, on a physical planet on Earth. This experiment was to raise the consciousness of all earth kingdoms, into self-consciousness.

The ***DEVIC*** overlord of earth is an entity called PAN, who agreed to the experiment, provided we honoured and respected its kingdoms. The ***ELEMENTALS*** are the workers or builders of form, under control of the Devic lords, on all physical planets, and man is seen as god, to them. Thought forms from the Elohim are directed to specific galaxies and planets - and on reaching them, they would precipitate to a planet over immeasurable eons of time. These thought forms would eventually transmute into the etheric/physical form. Over millions of years, electro- magnetic energy, gravity and attraction, would come into play, thereafter thought forms would transmute into physical form. This could only occur with full participation from the Devic kingdoms, who knew they were doing the fathers work.

The intention of divinity to send thought forms to a specific planet, is influenced by the Elohims desire to out-picture the supreme creators will, therefore Earth was the goal of the gods. At this juncture, I offer the reader a communication from a great being, who has given the group many incredible discourses about our solar system, and galaxy. AVON'S communication came through on the 14/11/85, when the group was taken on a visualization journey to a bio-space city craft, in Scorpio; ***At the heart of the Creator are vast seed thoughts. These seed thoughts are vast states of*** *consciousness, comprising universes of being. This power expresses itself outwards and individualizes further, becoming vast universes, and galaxies. The great lords of creation sent out their consciousness by refinement of individuality, then they would reach a solar system, and then - by further refinement, they reached the planets within those solar systems, on the inner planes of being.*

They expressed themselves into matter, projecting on an apparently never-ending spiral, seed thoughts of light into matter. Where a material worlds are concerned, these seed thoughts of matter, take millions, and millions, of years, to form. It is merely a thought that is projected into matter to see how it will respond, react and unite, with that matter harmoniously; it then sends it back to its source, as a perfect picture of that seed thought.

*The creators who sent out the seed thought - the Elohim, stand to one side to see how the experiment works; when it has been completed, they allow their prodigy to express their own creativity on other worlds of matter. Let us treat the planet as an entity - an experiment of consciousness in matter. Out in the *Mazzaroth* are many of your brothers and sisters, who have experienced consciousness in matter, but perhaps not the same way that you have.*

In this computerized space city, your brothers and sister of light from other star systems, and galaxies, monitor your progress of evolution, on your planet. The purpose of the space city that we are in, is to link the Mazzaroth mind, the solar mind, the planetary mind, and the individual mind, to the paradise worlds of the Creator, in the great universe of Kolob, so that the divine plan can be made clear to man.

The great central sun of Kolob can be visualized as a vast spiritual vortex of light, at the centre of all the universes. We are ONE with this sun, and have ever been so from the beginning, therefore Kolob is also within us. Over the years frequent references have been made about Kolob on our tapes, and it may interest the reader to know, that the only other references to it - outside of our tapes that I am aware of, comes from an Egyptian hieroglyph given to Joseph Smith, the founder of the Mormon church, by an Angel. There is a photograph of this hieroglyph in the Mormon bible, and I find it very interesting that from the hundreds of full-trance channel centres on earth at this time, none make any reference to the name of the great central sun; no doubt there is other information out there somewhere?

AREL came through in early 1977, to give this information about Kolob; ***You were with god in the beginning. A great star exploded, but before that you were one with god - with Kolob. In truth, you are a cell within a cell of god.***

RA AB HOUTEP gave the group this teaching about Kolob, on the 18/2/93; ***Please ask your questions, no matter how much they may seem to be irrelevant.***

(Amy; I've just read about the planet going into a null zone where all the energies are thrown out of balance, and also that the human body - as part of the planet are taking this on.) ***Yes that is so. You have been entering the null zone for a short while now. These energies come from Kolob, and you will find disturbances and a tendency towards fragmentation, in the world scene. Man was one with the supreme creator in the beginning, a cell within god. A cell within the great sun of Kolob, from whence the great fiat, of let there be light, emanated.***

Amazing discoveries have been made about the ATOM, in quantum mechanics, quantum Physics, and particle physics, and it is now accepted, that the physical atom, has an etheric/spiritual counterpart. Einstein's equation - E=MC squared, suggested that Energy = mass at the speed of light, which has interesting implications in relation to ASCENSION, and TRANSMUTATION. Physicists now know that energy and mass are one and the same; simplified, it must therefore be correct to say that energy can became mass, and mass can revert to energy.

This being the case, the spiritual and physical planes must also be inter-penetrable; divine mind has often said, as above so below, and vice versa. By raising the vibrations of the atoms of our physical bodies, during contemplation and meditation in love and light, we can **TRANSMUTE** our form back into light. The electron haze surrounding an atom seems to be the key factor, towards Ascension of physical form, back to light. It's interesting that the ancient Greeks called man Atoma, and Hindus call the soul of man Atma, are these coincidental references to man the soul, and man the atom? The Higgs Boson is being sought by physicists and scientists at the CERN particle accelerator, and also in the United States; in essence the Higgs boson is the 'cement' that binds atoms together creating the myriad forms that we see around us. They are trying to discover what 'mind' or force, bring together atomic particles that make a tree, a flower, the human body, etc? The simple answer is Prana - the holy breath, the life force, the mind of god, dark energy, etc. Physicists must first come to terms with the fact that the physical universe is a microcosm of the macrocosm - a spiritual universe, invisible to their instruments and human eyes. I believe a time is fast approaching when particle accelerators, will help them to understand, and realize this.

Divine mind says that energy follows thought, so what we give our attention to - or visualize, can or will manifest; there is now strong evidence to support this in modern metaphysical research. As embryonic gods, our thoughts and intentions go out, and can or will, create something, but not always pleasant, as the corporate human earth mind has shown with its wars, judgments, anger, and aggression.

Included below are a few discourses about thought, intention, and visualizations, going out as energy, and the effects that might come about, by these thoughts. KARATTA; ***Gradually, as you attune yourself to your new vibration, you will find that everything seems to centre itself in a thought world. You will find that you are communicating with nature, other beings, music, light, and all sorts of vibrations, in what you might term a thought world. When you return 'home'*** (Leave your physical body***) you suddenly realize that you move at the speed of thought.***

Gradually you discover that you can cover distances - if I can call them that, with instantaneous speed. You see, life enfolds itself in thought, whether you are in human form, or soul form. You have created many marvellous, beautiful, and wondrous things, in the world of the ethers. You created your heart's desire before your incarnation, by thought and intention.

JOHNNY; ***Your thoughts go out and collect other thoughts of the same vibration; so if you've had a bad day at the office, and became angry, then your thoughts will join other angry***

thoughts, as a black cloud of negativity. As more and more of these angry thoughts meet up, they create an atmosphere for something to happen, in the physical human mind world. And then something will happen!

ARCHANGEL MICHAEL gave this teaching, during a communication dated the 25/1/94;***Prana is pure spirit, an active force, that uplifts spirit. Use it by visualization - by soul breathing, to clear negativity; Visualize a pillar of light, and as energy follows thought, transmutation takes place, give attention to it, take the time to bring it into your body, in meditation.***

RA AB HOUTEP- 14/11/93; ***You express from the soul within. Your bodies are temples of light, yet man has destroyed the harmony in the physical, and astral realm, as energy follows his thoughts. Light channels are therefore working in the darkness, as beings of light.***

DWAAL KHUUL -12/6/75; ***Power comes to you through the open mind, . . you are able therefore - albeit unconsciously, to transmit from your head centre, all your desire for peace, and perfection, into the surrounding atmospheres of your world. As an initiate, your thought carries great power. This mind power by-passes human mind understanding.***

SIMON BAR SIMON, came through on the 25/8/77, to explain it, in his way; ***Whatever you desire, you can image into existence. Choose this day whom you will serve, and whatever you desire; there is nothing that you cannot have if you desire it, and according to what you desire, so do your deserts come to you.***(Divine humour) ***Simon will say but a blessing then; as love pours forth as a golden ray, mighty I AM presence, come forth in that which I visualize, and desire, as energy follows thought.***

It has been given by divine mind that pulsations/energy -from the Universes, back to Kolob, are called the in-breath of god. Pulsation from Kolob, are called the out-breath of god. On the in-breath of god, is all form drawn back to the source - by transmutation into pure spiritual Pranic energy? It has also been given that on the out-breath of god, let there be light, continues into the expanding voids of darkness. Could a black hole be a spiritual vortex into another dimension, or universe? On the out-breath of god, does the transmuted etheric/spiritual energy and thought, go out to create new universes, galaxies, and solar systems. Scientists agree that the horses head nebula near Orion's belt, is a new star field; if this is true, where did it come from?

Are black holes photon vortices that link Galaxies, and Universes? Scientists seem sure that everything entering a black hole apparently loses its light. I understand that a photon is a trapped light particle, and therefore invisible to the human eye. Did we lose our spiritual/etheric light bodies, during the in-breath of god, by some process known only to the Supreme Creator, when we arrived in the void of darkness, as consciousness beings?

I have given the reader many concepts from divine mind - using my human mind's under-standing of them, in relation to god, divinity, etc. I have tried to condense divine mind ancient wisdom/mystery teachings, from the Arel tapes and other sources into simple English language, which can never do justice to them. We can read, study, and contemplate divinity, but just when we think we've got the whole story, something else comes to our awareness, and its back to square one.

I have studied, meditated, read, listened, and re-listened to hundreds of my full trance tapes, covering innumerable subjects, at the deepest levels, and have finally realized, that the more I think I know about divinity, the less I really understand. It has been given on our tapes a number of times that, THE HUMAN MIND DOES NOT HAVE THE CAPACITY, TO FULLY UNDERSTAND DIVINE MIND.A beautiful quote on how to get in touch with our higher-self, was given by Arel, during a communication on the 17/5/79, and remains fixed in my mind; ***The mind will be able to grasp many things, when the heart begins to implement them.***

Where we came from, and how we got there in the first place, is incomprehensible to our human minds. As the reader considers the many full trance channelled messages within this book, it seems apparent that we may have arrived in the void from another universe, or unknown dimension, before Let there be Light.

I will finish off this chapter, with part of a beautiful full trance message from **AKHENATON,** concerning creation, and our involvement in it. This communication came through on the 28/6/1980; ***In this moment, we direct light to the world of man. Stir a-wake sons and daughters of light; let the rays from the great God - who is all light, and pure spirit, descend now upon you. May the eternal Sun, bestow upon you in this moment, its benediction and its blessing, for are you not that sun?***

Did you not before the beginning of all time - as man conceives of it with your father, create the worlds of matter? Where you not there before even the forms manifested themselves in the worlds of the ethers; did you not sing from the heart of first cause, when light breathed forth, into the darkness of un-creation?

Was that not your voice and your heart, which sang the glad hosanna, let there be light? Was that not you that went forth into all creation, singing the hymn of praise to the eternal sun, and father? Was that not you that entered into the depths and darkness of all creation, yet singing your song of love with your Creator? And did you not come up through all creation, singing the song of love, with your Creator?

Then arise children of light, cast from you the shackles which have bound you, and en-slaved you, into the worlds of illusion. Extend your hands to the sun of all light; be lifted up, oh children of light, and enter in upon the new City - the great illumination, the *Horizon of the Sun* and then together with deep love, and deep joy, raising your hands, say to this earth. .... Beloved son....... beloved child..... be you lifted up, even as I am lifted up. Behold the dawn of the eternal sun. Blessings and greetings... Akhenaton.

(* The Elohim are the seven creator lords of light)

(*Kolobis best understood as the centre where the will of god is known. It is the centre of creation – the big bang, an etheric vortex of light influencing all the universes galaxies,etc. It is also called the great central sun.)

(* The Shakina, is our pure spiritual light body.)

(*Our Merkabah vehicle enables us to travel inter-dimensionally at the speed of though between galaxies and universes. It is the 'glue' that enables us to create vast etheric biospheres of light (space cities, craft, ufo's, etc)

(*The Mazzaroth are our Zodiac houses - and beyond, into the Cosmos.)

(* The Devic lords are advanced entities involved in the worlds of creation. They do the bidding of the Elohim, bringing thought forms into physical manifestation. They are responsible to their elemental workers – understood as nature spirits.)

(* The horizon of the Sun* was the name of Akhenaton's city at Amana. Akhenaton was Pharaoh of Egypt in the 18th dynasty. He left Karnak to build his new city and re-introduced the concept of one god, because the Egyptians had lost this original truth, and were worshipping many gods; Akhenaton was maligned in ignorance by those that followed him - including modern historians. He is an Avatar, and in his last embodiment was physically both man and women, but notwithstanding this, he sired children!)

Chapter 4

THE FISHERMAN

Our Saturday morning meetings became known as the gathering of light group, which initially comprised seven of us. We met in unconditional love, and light, and some of the group had been friends for many years. I could be considered the new-comer, but everyone was happy to hold the meetings at my house; it was my custom to clean and prepare the lounge prior to everyone's arrival. I cut flowers to decorate the Altar, select a channelled tape, and meditation music, etc. My own simple routine for grounding the energy before we met was to light the main altar oil light, and then an incense stick; photographs of Swami, and Jesus, were the main centrepiece of our altar. Two other candles - representing love and light, would be lit once our gathering started.

Within a month of our group forming, and as soon as everyone was seated, a beautiful rose perfume permeate the lounge; at first I thought it was a strong perfume, that one of the ladies was wearing, and that it was only me who was aware of it, but this was not the case. We all tried to rationalize its origin but eventually we just accepted that it was especially for our group, from divine mind. During this time Joan and I were in regular contact with Amy and George, but try as we might to arrange a time for a visit to Johannesburg, it never happened. I was particularly sad for Joan, for I had already been down to see them twice, yet she had never met them face to face; we recalled Johnny's communication to us when he said; ***Well...... we might get together again...... who knows?***

Occasionally, Amy would ask Johnny for a message for us in Bulawayo, and one such communication came through on the 9/12/93; ***Know that we are with you, and know that your families are guided, guarded, and protected...... use your ring pass not to individually protect them. Don't worry about what their human minds fail to grasp, and don't allow yourself to be***

pressurized by anyone either; when they approach you with that leer that you know very well, or when they say, 'I feel that'.....(Laugher) ***then put your ring pass not around yourself.***

(Amy; Johnny, especially for Bob and Joan, do you have something also?) ***Yes we will do that for them...... Let it be a cleansing experience that comes into their lives, at this particular time; it's a glorious time that comes with the birth of the Christ child consciousness, peace on earth and goodwill to all men. We bless both Bob, and Joan, and those that you bring into your hearts, and minds at this time.***

As the years passed Joan and I began to feel more isolated and out of touch with Amy and George; we only received the occasional tape or letter from them. It seemed Amy, and George, had continuing medical problems, which made a firm visiting time difficult. Our human minds craved for regular confirmation or verbal channelled support from the Arel centre, that we were doing the correct work. It was important for Joan and my-self especially, because we were part of the five star group on earth. Over the years, occasional confirmation came through from Johannesburg that Johnny was in touch with us, on the inner planes.

We received another message from Johnny, which came on the 28/7/95; ***I'm going to be returning again to the inner planes for a while, but know...... I am with you always. From time to time we will be able to chatter a bit, and give my brother*** (The Channel) ***a rest for a while. We are working with him, and he needs a little bit of rest, this is also why I've come this time, to do a bit of re-adjustment. Also our other brother, and sister.... who are not present in your physical home at this time - those to the North you. We send them our deep love, and also the message, lo I am with you always.***

(Dr; In consciousness, Johnny?) ***Yes......We bless the work that they do up there in their land,...... we bless it in love, in light, and in truth, as it unfolds and deepens, bringing a greater awareness to all those up North, where a great future - spiritually, is waiting to unfold. In this moment let us also attune with Swami Sathya Sai Baba. Consciously attune now,***

because we are aware of incarnate deity. Swami is the answer to the prayer that has gone out for centuries of time.

Joan and I had been meeting regularly on Tuesday mornings, during which we shared the latest information received from many contacts world-wide. I attended her Emissary of Divine light, attunements most Thursday evenings, becoming close friends with her School of truth, Emissary, and Yoga family. One Tuesday morning Joan was reading to me from a newly released book; the information was presented in such a way that I found myself saying yes! yes, at the end of each paragraph. I had total affinity with every word that left her lips triggering something deep within me.

Suddenly I gasped as a violent pain shot across the top of my head - between the pineal and pituitary charkas; I recall putting my hands to my head and moaning softly, Joan jumped up and put her hand on my shoulder, asking what was wrong, and expressing concern for me. I did not know. Despite the discomfort, I laughed because the stabbing pain was not unbearable; eventually I took my hands away from my head trying to explain what was happening,

From the top-centre of my head a warm opening sensation was taking place. It felt like my head was opening up, from the centre outwards, as if my skull was opening. I put my hands up to my head, to make sure that the top of my head was still in place, trying to explain to Joan what was happening, between laughing and groaning.

The energy and empowerment was amazing; one moment I would be laughing, and the next gasping, as the pleasurable yet mild aching numbness continued. Joan sat next to me, holding my hand, and gradually the dull pain eased, but not the numbness. The top of my head felt like it was open to the elements - as if my skull was no longer there, but of course it was.

Eventually I got up needing to walk around the garden; everything was extremely bright, vibrant, and clear. The flowers and trees stood out starkly, and also the sky, the clouds, everything. I said to Joan, 'everything is so bright, it hurts my eyes to look at things'. We went to my car to get my dark glasses and it felt like I was gliding over the ground, as if I didn't have a body, I look down at my feet, just to make sure. We returned to the veranda and sat down, then Joan went off to make some fresh tea; she said 'now you just stay there and relax don't move'. We grinned at each other, and it crosses my mind that maybe she thinks I'll disappear in a puff of smoke, or something?

I continue breathing in huge gulps of air…. and felt incredible. The top of my head felt wide open - yet it wasn't? I was conscious of a powerful energy, and yet a numb-ness. I was uncertain what was happening to me, but gradually my breathing became more regular, and then a feeling of incredible empowerment, as if nothing was all that important anymore.

We had some more tea and discussed what had happened, then we sat quietly together for some time, and then I needed to walk around the garden again. The colours and energy around me, were amazing, but then I realized that I must get back to the office for an appointment. I wondered how I was supposed to drive a car, with the top of my head apparently missing? We walked to my car, but everything is surreal; I'm not quite in the car, and yet I am. On the way back to work, I pulled in at a lay-bye, to try and focus my mind.

The opening of my third eye - or whatever it was, remained with me for three days, especially the numbness. During this time, I had many vivid dream recalls of Egypt, and other incarnate earth experiences. Gradually everything returned to normal. Interestingly, as I write of these events, that energy and numbness returns to my head - but only slightly. Shortly after this event, I became very involved in the physical universe again, as my marriage had broken up.

The Emissaries of Divine Light were holding their annual congress at the Gwaai river hotel, so Joan and I were very busy picking up delegates from the airport, and arranging overnight accommodation; there was also a lot of activity and planning, with Harold and Louise. Eighty delegates from all over the world attended this event but as sometimes happens, there was dissention in the ranks between the two South African delegations. They could not agree which province should be the headquarters, of the E.D.L. in their country; the situation was very human mind centred, and childish, but had to be sorted out. A special session was arranged by the EDL leader, Michael Exeter in the hope of reaching a compromise.

Joan and I were not interested in attending, so we decided to go for a walk along the Gwaai river valley, instead. It was late February, and the many species of Acacia trees were in full bloom; we walked slowly - in one-ness, looking at the different wild animal spoor, that were clearly visible on the rain swept sandy pathways. The bush was lush with vegetation, and we stopped every now and again, to compare knowledge of the different flowers, and trees. We walked, talked, and laughed, happy in each-others company, on a warm sunny day.

Our special afternoon was soon over, and we arrived back the hotel just before dusk. We sat around the swimming pool, and shortly afterwards Harold and our Bulawayo friends, joined us. Gladys told us that Michael Exeter had handled the situation very well, and it appeared to be resolved. They excused themselves in preparation for supper. Joan and I decided to go into the conference room, to anchor the vibes in love, and light. The conference room was in darkness, and we could not find the light switch; my lighter and a candle, resolved that problem. We sat opposite each other, with the lighted candle on a table between us. I remember calling in Archangel Michael, Jesus and Swami, and then;

I was in Egypt, in a military uniform; a young woman was walking with me, as we approached a clearing, amongst the trees. We were holding hands, she wore a plain brown tunic and was partly Nubian; olive skinned, with glossy black hair. We were very much in love, but my role in the Pharaoh's army, made it difficult for me to be with her as much as we would have liked. She was the daughter of the village headman - a disciple of light….. but she was also Joan?

Her village was in Southern Khaam, (Egypt) just below the rapids, where my boats had been anchored for the night. The clearing was swept clean, and a small fire, was burning,…… we sat on a log that was shiny with use, embraced, then kissed. I wanted her so much, as I fondled her body. She jumped up laughing and said, 'now you behave'! She threw her arms around my neck, gradually sliding them down my back, and pulling me close to her, at the hips teasing me. You temptress! I said, as she jumped away laughingly, then she became very serious. 'We have the whole night together and you will be tired of me in the morning'.

I was about to respond, but she put her finger on my lips and said 'you know I'm teasing you'. She said 'how long will you be with me this time'. I wasn't sure, and felt bad that I couldn't tell her of my campaign, for it was vital that we crossed the Nile to a rendezvous point in the east, without anyone knowing about it, I had not even told my men! I explained as best I could, assuring her our marriage would go ahead as planned, and that the Pharaoh himself, would be there to bless us. Only one more campaign my beloved I promise you, and then you will move to Memphis with me. She snuggled close to me, whispering please be careful.

A whistle from a grove of trees behind us, announced that one of her servants had brought food, refreshments, and blankets for us, also a beautiful woven reed sleeping mat. I woke up as the faint light of dawn was colouring the horizon got dressed and kissed her on the cheek,….. she whimpered, but I had to go…… I felt guilty as I left her sleeping.

Where am I?....... Darkness?……I'm confused and disorientated…… Oh, Yes! I was sitting in the conference room with Joan, and we were meditating……. But where's Joan? Joan, where are you? A soft voice in front of me, in the darkness said, 'I'm here'. Joan what happened?...... She laughed and said, 'the candle went out'; it was at that point that the above memories came flooding back. We left the conference room and walked back to the swimming pool area, looking at each other, grinning and giggling. We ordered a drink from a passing waiter, who must have doubted our sanity, as we continued talking excitedly and laughing about what had just transpired between us. I said to Joan, 'Were you with me just now in Egypt?' She smiled, and nodded her head.

The waiter brought our drinks, and then Joan suddenly jumped to her feet and said, I'll bring you down to earth. She started waving her hands above my head, then down towards my feet, giggling all the time; in the middle of this grounding exercise, one of the delegates walked outside with his partner, looked at us and stopped in their tracks. They said something to each other, and then beat a hasty retreat back to the lounge. It must have looked ridiculous, a grown lady apparently waving her arms in supplication to some guy sitting on a chair; well that was it, we couldn't stop laughing. Shortly afterwards, Louise, and Gladys joined us.

We were still laughing, and talking excitedly, and they wanted to know what was so funny. We smiled looked at each other and Joan said, 'now don't be nosey', and then in a more serious note, 'I'll tell you later after dinner, we must go and get changed and have a bath. Now I knew what Joan had been referring to many years prior when she said, 'You left me in Egypt a long time ago, and I never saw you again'. I do not know what happened after I joined my men at the river. Over the years, many beings who came through spoke about the importance of Rhodesia, and Southern Africa generally, in relation to the unfolding new age of love and light. One communication in 1975, was from CECIL JOHN RHODES, he said; ***And if we can take your Rhodesia - if I may use that name, the new age of love, and light, will blossom forth from this great Southern African centre, pointing a way forwards for the rest of mankind.*** As I type these words - in the year 2011, I wonder when this occur, in view of what has transpired in Zimbabwe, since independence! On another tape Johnny said; ***Rhodesia and Southern Africa will become a conglomeration of separate states, which hold the key to a quantum leap forwards in consciousness, for mankind.***

An unusual event occurred in Zimbabwe, which relates directly to other sections of this book, and merits mention. In mid September 1994, a vast light appeared in the skies over western Zimbabwe at about 9.15 p.m. in the evening, and was seen by many people. The object was long, and oval shaped, and was surrounded by moving smaller lights. It was widely reported to be directing powerful spotlights to earth, which lit up the countryside. It was viewed from as far west as Francistown town in Botswana, to Kwe Kwe in Zimbabwe a distance of nearly 275 miles from its flight path just East of Bulawayo.

The first time that our group became aware of it was from TV news flashes and radio reports. The next day headlines in the local Bulawayo newspaper, reported that a large object had been seen in the skies, over Western Zimbabwe. During the next three days, reports came flooding in, to national television, and radio, concerning first hand sightings; it seemed that the meteorological office in Bulawayo were the only ones who thought it was a meteor shower. So what did people see in the skies over Bulawayo that night?

A friend of mine was driving past the Ascot racecourse, and pulled over when she first saw the object in the sky, she said; Bob it was heading Southward's… it was awe inspiring, very big and silent. It was very bright with objects going into it, and circling around it; we viewed it for about 12 seconds. Bob, it lit up the surrounding countryside beneath it as it glided towards the Nyamandhlovu farming area. Anyone who says it was a meteor shower is nuts!

A relative of mine who lived on a farm in the Nyamandhlovu valley was sitting on the veranda of their house, when; The whole sky lit up, and we rushed outside to see what was happening. Uncle Bob it was huge, silent, and very beautiful; it seemed to have three huge spotlights shining down to earth which lit up the whole valley… and smaller spotlights seemed to be moving around it. It headed Southwards and then it disappeared after about 10 seconds. I asked if it looked like a meteor shower, and she said, 'Uncle Bob I've never seen a meteor shower, but it seemed as if it was being driven… it was controlled, and seemed to be very big and high up'. Many other reports came in from different sources during the unfolding weeks, and most of them questioned the 'Met' office report.

The day after the sighting another strange event unfolded at a junior school in the midlands, which also received wide media coverage. This event was researched by a T.V. presenter called Jill Darke who ran a Saturday morning program called the Age of Aquarius, covering astrology and other esoteric subjects. She confirmed the press reports that children were playing on the field during break-time when two UFO's landed in a field next to the school boundary; apparently the children suddenly went very quiet which alerted a gardener. He saw two or three 'Greys', leaving one of the craft and walking towards the boundary fence of the school. A teacher also became aware that the children had suddenly quietened and, looking out the window, saw the craft and the ET's. She alerted the rest of the staff who quickly called the children into the classrooms. The 'Greys' got back into their craft and took-off, but not before a farmer - who was driving past, almost turned over his Vanette as a low level UFO passed over the road in front of him about 20ft above the ground. All of this might appear like science fiction, but I can assure the reader that these events were very real - so much so that, people in dark suits arrived from the U.K and America within two days of the occurrence!

Jill Dark and the head mistress asked the children to draw pictures of what they had seen. They resembled the conventional small bodied, large headed, black eyed, ET's. The children's pictures were shown on local and international TV screens but I never learnt of the outcome of these unofficial investigations. According to our tapes, contact has been made with certain governments by craft of the legions of light, but sadly, it seems that they are only interested in the technology behind them as a means of gaining dominance over other countries. How sad.

The following communication concerning Governments secretive attitude to UFOs, was given to the group by AVON on the 10/12/92; ***Earth is in contact with kindred star systems which are your brothers and sisters in this galaxy. The dark powers are fleeing as our friends and their craft are nearing earth and the experiment comes to its final conclusion. Scout ships of the light have made contact with your earth leaders but they seek only alliances with us as a means of world control. The light beyond Jupiter - a glow in the heavens - has been seen by your scientists, but they have suppressed the information.***

Friends of one of our group knew a teacher from the school in question, so phoned her to confirm - or deny, what was being said. She confirmed that she had seen the 'Grey's' and their craft clearly, as had 18 adults - both black and white, and also 38 children. Everyone confirmed seeing similar things - with slight variations, at the school that day. She also confirmed that she had agreed to be interviewed by foreign investigators, and had given them her account. As a result of this sighting and events surrounding it, I phoned Amy asking if she could get a comment from Avon, or Johnny, as to what had occurred that night, and also at the school the following day.

The following communication from Ra ab Houtep, came through on the 22nd of September 1994; ***Greetings and blessing, welcome, yes. What shall we talk about?***

(Amy; Beloved One if I may ask, somebody has requested your information on a giant spaceship that was seen over Zimbabwe about 10 days ago. They wanted to know what the indications are of this.

Lots of people saw it. It wasn't just a strange occurrence?) ***No it wasn't. Coming as it did in the period of Virgo and approaching the time of the descending Christ spirit - and the angelic forces and powers - it was an outward manifestation - a space city which materialized it-self in the planetary ethers in order to herald the powers coming in with this period that you are entering into now. This is but one of many; we have said to you, there will be visitors appearing in your skies and to watch for them. These are forerunners of a great mission to planet earth.***

(Amy; This is wonderful.) ***Yes a great mission to planet Earth... you will see more and more of them. There are many more people incarnate now who are attuning themselves with the divine unity concept, thereby emanating a spirit of love, brotherhood, and service, so that these visitors - in this particular case Regulus through Spica, will be able to make physical contact with your planet. The atmospheres of welcome, understanding, and acceptance, have grown. This is something you can work towards, during this particular period you are in now, and then, watch your skies again.***

(Amy; This is wonderful beloved teacher. Was the mission of that particular ship to see how far man has come or just to show themselves, so that we can become aware?) ***To show them-selves so that you could become aware, Yes! But they could not have shown themselves had the 'climate'*** (The awakening awareness of mankind) ***upon the planet not been ready for it. It is because of the heightening of spiritual consciousness and awareness upon your planet that a number of these space cities are able to reveal themselves in your atmospheres.***

(Amy; We are living in wonderful times.) ***Yes, there shall be signs and wonders in the heavens - say your scriptures not so? When you have contacted God as a living within-ness, then you have no need of outward stimulation; seek God within you... identify with God within. This is the message of your incarnate Avatar who says, find God within and His righteousness - the word he uses is 'Dharma'- will be added unto you.***

During the next few weeks further information came through about the 'space city'; piecing everything together, it appears it was first seen over Lake Kariba moving southwards to the Zimbabwe boarder with South Africa where it disappeared. Two friends of mine at Gweru - about 120 miles from Bulawayo, said it was in view for about10 to 12 seconds, going towards the South, when it disappeared.

In February 1995, I was fishing in a competition at Olive Beadle camp at the extreme western end of Lake Kariba when the subject of the 'thing in the sky' was raised. I listened fascinated to two members of our fishing club - who had seen the whole thing, related their stories; 'We had just finished our braai, (barbeque) and were sitting outside having a beer, when a small brilliant white light appeared in the sky in the direction of Milibizi (about 50 miles away). As we watched, it grew larger and larger and brighter. It then became an oval shape. It was huge and the hills beneath it stood out clearly as lights shone down towards the ground. It started moving towards Bulawayo and there were small lights moving around it and in it. All in all, we watched it for about half a minute. We couldn't believe what we were seeing… It was amazing'.

Amy phoned me from Johannesburg shortly after the sightings and told me that they had asked Johnny about the 'Grey's' and their craft, to which he said; ***Wherever light manifests, the dark lords will seek to make their presence felt, in order to keep humanity in fear.***

On a fishing trip to Mpala Jena camp - above the Victoria falls, I had another out of body experience for over half an hour. It was usual for me to get away by myself on fishing trips, where I enjoyed the peace, solitude, and at-one-ment, with nature. Fishing was quiet that morning and I remember gazing at the water where my lines entered it, and then looking at my watch and making a mental note that I'd give it-a-go for an hour and then make some tea. Leaning forwards on my chair - elbows on my knees, I concentrated on any line movement.

The breeze created small ripples that danced between my fishing lines, and sunlight produced iridescent flashes of colour on the water surface. My fishing Buddy Johnny Hansen who had passed on a year prior, came strongly into my mind, and then I sensed a presence on my right and said laughingly Johnny, what the hell are you doing here; you haven't got a body, so how are you going to catch fish? I sensed his chuckle and heard some cryptic comment - a telepathic communication.

I gazed back into the water watching my lines, nothing was biting; and then - if in a dream state, I came back from somewhere? I looked at my wrist watch and realized that three quarters of an hour had passed! Leaning back in my chair, fear suddenly gripped me, I said aloud, you idiot Bob! My human mind had clicked in, and I realized how careless I'd been. I wondered if I had nodded off; there I was, sitting on a sandbar on the banks of the Zambezi River fishing, in crock infested waters, totally switched off to the potential dangers of lion, and elephant. And then - as if I was watching a film, everything came flooding back to me.

A hippo had surfaced in mid river, snorted, then headed upstream; a small heard of elephant had come down to drink on the opposite side of the stream, less than 50 meters from me. A small crock had left the river, and moved up the stream in front of me, about 15 feet away. Everything slowly came back to me - as if I was watching a movie. I remember the squawking of Egyptian geese, and watching the African Jacanas, playing in the reeds on the far bank. I realize that once again in my life I had been totally in command and aware of everything that was happening around me, and yet I was somewhere else? I had been in two places at once for ¾ of an hour but my human mind had been un-aware of it at the time.

I continued to keep Thursday evenings free to meditate and link with the Johannesburg group. I would sit quietly in the lounge, candles ablaze on the altar with soft abstract music playing. One evening - in deep meditation, I became aware of flames reflecting through the fanlight window somewhere outside, I rushed out expecting to find the house next door on fire, but there was nothing visible. I looked over the wall, then up the road, but nothing was on fire. I returned to the lounge very confused. On reflection, I could not understand why the flames were only evident in the fanlight window and not the main windows. I am at a loss to understand what this event meant, or was telling me.

During this period of my life, I was to experience other unusual phenomena. I have already mentioned that I played a lot of sport and enjoyed social interactions with my friends, at diverse levels. I was chairman of a large sports club where I coached rugby and played bowls. I also belonged to two fishing clubs where I was an active fisherman. A group of my close bowling friends used to meet every Friday evening at the bowls club to unwind after the working week was over. One evening I sat quietly by myself at the corner of the bar, half listening to various conversations, when I exteriorized again. It was a strange sensation; it seemed I moved backwards, and outwards; as this happened, everyone and everything in the bar seemed to become miniaturized. It seemed that I was very far away looking down on everything and everyone. I heard a far off voice saying, Bob, Bob! Where are you? I returned to my body with a bump!

On another occasion, I woke up at about 3.00 a.m. and sat up in bed, a clear vision etched in my mind`s eye. The Earth was engulfed in flames...... then gradually the vision changed, the Earth was in silhouette - a black ball in space, with millions of stars in the background. A huge entity was standing on Earth, legs astride, also in silhouette. This entity was surrounded by an electric blue halo. In its right hand was a silver sword - held aloft, surrounded by gold and white shafts of light, radiating out to the cosmos. The vision slowly faded. I sensed the entity was Archangel Michael, but cannot be sure.

Chapter 5

THE AVATAR

The Johannesburg group would continue to query information about Swami, clinging fearlessly to their love for Jesus. Many question and answer sessions were to take place, between divine mind, and human mind.

On the 18/11/94 (during a thunderstorm) AVON gave additional information on Sai Baba. ***At this time – the time of the incarnate Avatar, these powers are mightily increased, for they earth themselves through the Avatar so to speak. The Avatars message at this point, is to personalize the cosmic message, and bring the affairs of the mental world, into man's experience. The great transforming powers of transmutation – that is within you, is less than perfect, but will become perfect, It is very relevant at this time, that light channels put one, and one, together,***(a crash of thunder) ***to re-align the spiritual impulses, that come thundering*** (divine humour) ***from cosmos.***

You are energizing, and being energized by, the incarnate Avatar, Swami Sai Baba, in consciousness. Avon does not wish to say a great deal at this time, except that you are working with the Avatar energies of Pisces, and the fire energies of Scorpio. This will bring about a tremendous power of rebirth, in your world…. move with it, you are part of it, you are disciples in it. There will always be challenges entering your lives that will test your ego. You must learn to merge with the Christ of yourselves.

Great, great, great, is the power which grows at this time. Your newly discovered Ashram, in the great sub-continent of India, extends its tremendous love to you….. it's recognition of you….. It's knowledge of you, and its inclusiveness of you. At this time we join together as one cosmic family. Let the Christ-feast, or mass, begin now. We seed the lights shining in the

great mountains, and hear the chants of holy-ness, we see the great heart of love (The incarnate Avatar of love)

On the 23rd of November - Swami's 70th Birthday, it was Bulawayo's turn to host his national birthday celebrations; the Hindu Vashee hall was full of devotees from all over Zimbabwe, Zambia, and South Africa. I had made careful notes of my address to the congregation, which was to be followed by a half hour channelled message about the Avatar that had just arrived from Johannesburg.

We had lunch of traditional Hindu cuisine, and met two new arrivals to Bulawayo - Bent and Beta Kristensen, who had been devotees of Swami for over 20 years; they were from Denmark and had retired 5 years earlier. The Krisensen's expressed a desire to Swami, that they would like to work in his name, and Swami said, ***yes this will happen.*** They were drawn to Bulawayo via a message from the Central African Sai Baba headquarters in Kenya. Swami's will would be done, as so often happens, in apparently mystical ways?

It was a beautiful evening of entertainment; Bhajan's, dancing, and personal anecdotes about Swami were revealed, and all too soon it was my turn to address the gathering. I was a little bit nervous, as there were about 500 people in the hall. Kiran introduced me, and gave a brief overview of our group, after which I was called up to the stage. I gave a tape to the sound controller then took out my notes spreading them on the lectern. I intoned the Aum three times and everyone joined in.

I turned to look at a large full frontal photograph of Swami on the stage, a powerful energy of love flooded my body, and mind...... I remember mumbling, I am pleased to be here in my body, and then I don't think I looked at my notes again. I was somewhere behind and above my body, yet in it, a strange but empowered feeling. Something? ….. an energy, was on the stage with me on my left? On recall, I remember speaking about some of the deeper truths about Swami and his incredible sacrifice in incarnating. I pointed out that as an Avatar, he did not need to incarnate through woman but had only done so to show us that we too are God. I told them that he chose to incarnate into the Hindu faith to restore the ancient Vedic truths and teachings given nearly 10,000 years earlier.

I said Swami is not a Hindu Avatar and then briefly returned to my conscious mind as those gathered in the hall gasped in disbelief. I emphasized that Sathya Sai Baba was a world Avatar pointing out that from the Bible and Christian perspectives he was in truth, The lord God of hosts or the ever coming one as referred to in the Bible and Torah. I didn't remember very much more at the time except that Kiran and three other older Hindu committee members sitting in the front row were staring intently at me and then to my right.

Suddenly there was loud clapping and I realized that I had been talking to a hall full of people... I mumbled thank you and started to walk off the stage when Kiran indicated that I should stay. I was confused as he shouted something to me... I was not sure what was happening, so continued to walk off again. He met me by the curtains and said, 'Bob what about the tape?'I walked back to the rostrum and gave a mumbled briefing on the entity who would be talking, then I met Kiran behind the stage curtains and asked him, what had happened? He smiled at me and said, 'I'll tell you later.' I took the opportunity to go outside for a cigarette, and also to clear my mind, and recall what had happened.

Slowly and clearly, everything came back to me, it was like watching a film in my mind. I remembered being on the stage, totally empowered, and in control. Eventually I recalled everything that I had said, and yet it wasn't Bob talking. I clearly recalled my discourse, and the look on the faces of the audience, to certain things that I'd said, so why did it feel so strange? Returning to the hall, Kiran came and sat next to me and said, 'Who was that standing next to you on the stage, . . . four of us saw an entity….. a white etheric form on your left? I don't know if anyone else saw it'. I explained to him that I had been aware of something next to me but hadn't seen anything. He laughed, patted me on the shoulder, then returning to his seat, he said I'll see you at the end of the celebration.

The Aarti ceremony was starting; several small candles on a salver, with burning camphor, are offered to Swami in a circular motion, honouring Swami as God; thereafter they are offered to those present, merging us as one with God. The- burning of camphor - which is fragrant, white and pure, is symbolic of the soul. At the end of the ceremony, Joan came over to me smiling,(women sit separately from the men during all prayer meetings) we hugged and then she said, 'Wow, that was quite a speech'. I laughed and said I don't remember much about it.

Kelpenar Hari joined us and gave me a big hug, then said, you were guided by Swami this evening. We chatted to Kiran, and some of the other Sai devotees. It had been a lovely evening, as we mingled and were introduced to the other delegates. The chairman of the Sai Baba organization from Harare, asked if I could give a talk to the Sai group in Harare, I promised to come back to him. I remembered that he had been sitting in the front row next to Kiran, during my speech. He drew my attention because of the intensity of his eye contact with me, as I was talking.

We were offered vibhuuti then said our good-byes. Kiran walked to the car with us and put a note in my pocket as Kelpenar's sons came running out shouting, 'Uncle Bob, Uncle Bob.' They hugged us then knelt at my feet and touched them. I said, 'No, don't do that.' Kiran laughed and said, 'Bob, it's a Hindu custom to honour a divine being'. I said, 'But we're all divine, Kiran.' They just laughed and said, 'Uncle Bob we love you and are giving you Swami's blessings'. I took Joan home, stopping for coffee with her and Rod.

I went home in a very reflective mood; I was living by myself at the time and sat quietly in the lounge considering the evening's events and the talk that I'd given. I was still surprised at everything that had happened that evening, realizing that I was far from perfect and, once again, analysing myself and questioning my worthiness. I remembered the note that Kiran had put in my shirt pocket, it read; 'Message to your group. You that are immersed in light - which is the energy of love, who have taken the time, which is a gift conferred to us from light of Christ; to recognize this fact you should now embark on a mission to spread, and encircle, all in this light, just by the work you are already carrying out. Your group leader – uncle Bob, has been conferred with the necessary energy, and elevation required for this, because of his recent experience at the Ajna Chakra.(The opening of my pineal chakra.) Your group has the perfect leader who is tuned in for this Avatar's task of bringing light to all.

Beta and Bent returned to Denmark to sort out their affairs and make plans for a new life in Africa. They had decided to open an orphanage for children outside of Bulawayo in an area called the Matopos. The AIDS situation in Zimbabwe was deteriorating rapidly and many orphaned children were being looked after by their extended families who could barely feed themselves after 3 years of drought. Coincidentally - whilst the Kristensens were away, the Sai group had also been thinking about a food supply scheme in the same area and were making their plans as well. Synchronicity? No! An Avatar is all knowing.

We were soon to have other regular members of our Saturday morning meetings. Bent was a humble man - a 'doer', and an engineer, prior to his retirement. He loved Swami in his own way, but it was Beta who really understood Swami, being more able to relate to him, and the deeper truths of our tapes. Beta had been 'called' by Swami many years before, and had been privileged to have several interviews with him, over the years. Her son had also met Swami years before, and during that visit, Swami had manifested a ring for him. Bent and Beta had experienced many amazing manifestations by Swami, and had gained incredible insights into his divinity.

Shortly after Swami's birthday celebrations, I received a transcript from Amy. Herewith parts of a communication, explaining the Christ and the Avatar. It was channelled on the 20th of November, 1994 by RA AB HOUTEP; ***Believest thou not, that I am in the father, and the father is in me. The words that I speak unto you, I speak not of myself, it is the father that dwelleth within, that doeth the work. This is the lord Christ, referring to the indwelling of the Christ, not the words of an Avatar, claiming to be the incarnation.***

(Amy; Swami said that he was the one who sent Jesus) ***The lord Jesus himself, did not claim to be an Avatar, he was the son of god, He did not claim to be god incarnate; 'Believeth thou not that I am in the father, and the father is in me'. He did not say I AM the father. At one stage he said, I and the father are one, but that was a state of attainment. We will have to talk around this point gently for you, Remember that the lord Christ Jesus, was indwelt by the Christ. The Christ overshadowed and indwelt him, at the baptism in the river Jordan, in the 30th year of his life; it was an indwelling from the lord Christ - the Atma. You do*** *not have to surrender any of your beliefs, or love of the master Jesus, for in reality, there is no difference.*

The incarnate Avatar has come at this time to a different world, into a nation of people who have had previous Avatars within their soul group, and experience. This has made of them, the oldest spiritual nation in the world. The time has now come where spiritual strength in man's world, has become necessary for man's survival upon his planet..... so the incarnate Avatar incarnated as the whole Akashic record, for the whole world, in order to bring man, and god together, in divine unity, and consciousness. The very power of this incarnate Avatar, has attracted people from all over the world of man.

(Amy; What is the meaning of the term Avatar. You say that Jesus was overshadowed by the Christ?) *The Christ overshadowed, but did not incarnate in Jesus, he said so. All the evidence is in your Bible,..... but the difference at this time, is that the Christ incarnated consciously, into the present Avatar. The Avatar is a unique incarnate energy, which has come at this time, through Sri Sathya Sai Baba - the incarnate Avatar, to prepare those who wait for their ever-coming one. Your traditions lie deep in your subconscious mind, in your belief systems, between the east, and west. Hold dear in your heart your love for your beloved Jesus, it will not in any way effect your contact with the incarnate Avatar. Jesus was not an Avatar, but the Christ was the Avatar,.... the Christ in Jesus, did not incarnate, it overshadowed him..*

The Christ was the avatar, but the Jesus cult - worship in the western world today, is drawing man away from the fact that, 'I and the father are one'. Man is the divine unity with god, not separate from god. As you worship the Christ, attune yourself with the Atma,– which is the essence of your incarnate Avatar, for he also says, I am in you, and you are in me. You need have no sense of separation of difference. The world is able to accept, an incarnate Akashic Avatar, but it was not so 2000 years ago, for the world as a whole was unknown to people of 2000 years ago. Tribes and nations, were even more barbaric, and uncivilized then, than they are at present. Your present day

communication systems make it possible for your incarnate Avatar, to reach every corner of the globe, in presence and spirit. 2000 years ago, this could not have happened.

(Amy; Sai could not have incarnated 2000 years ago, because his presence would have shattered the toucher, and physical) ***Yes, but now he can, and has, and when the lord Christ Jesus returns - reappears, he will be seen in the glorious majesty of the Christ.***

(Amy; Yes in that sense they are twin brothers) ***Oh yes, Of the same soul. Sai says, do not look at this little form that I occupy, as the incarnate Avatar. The master Jesus said, why callest thou me good, don't look at my form you don't know me. He who sent me, has seen the father, but he was not referring to the form. In your new testament, you can discern between the times Jesus was speaking, and when the Christ spoke through him. It has taken your Christian church, three centuries, to come to the point of trying to understand, who Christ Jesus really was.***

In the previous chapter on the Avatar, I related events that occurred at Vas and Bharti Patel's house, but that was not to be the end of it! You will recall that the 24 hour devotional alter, had been set up between the dining room French-doors, and the outside garage. A large tarpaulin gave protection from the sun; it was a beautiful altar, with palms, flowers, a painting of Shiva, and a statue of Sai Baba of Shirdi, Swami, and other Hindu deities. There was a large chair for Shiva - a traditional Hindu offering for Shiva to visit his devotees, with a beautiful embroidered rug over it; in addition, two large lotus flower design prayer carpets covered the concrete flooring in front of the alter.

At about 3.15 p.m. on the Saturday, a shaft of sunlight shone through a small hole in the tarpaulin falling at the feet of Swami's statue. Kiran took photographs of it, because the golden/white ray of light was coincidental, yet meaningful to him, and the devotees. Two weeks later his children were acting in a school Christmas play at the theatre club, in Bulawayo. He took his camera along, which had six remaining exposures on it. The play was called how Jesus loves you. Whilst watching it he said to himself, 'Swami they are talking in your name - the name of Love, show them a miracle'. His children came on stage and he took photographs of them, using up the rest of spool. In the morning he dropped the spool off for developing.

Kiran phoned me ten days before Christmas, as he wanted to show me the photographs; he arrived with some of the devotees, and put 8 large photographs on the table. Four were of the shrine, and four of the theatre club production; the first photograph was a full frontal picture of the shrine, the second was a photograph of the shaft of sunlight, falling at the feet of Swamis statue. The remaining two photographs were different views of the altar. To the left of the statue was Shiva's chair, and above the chair - where a blanket had been hung to hide a doorway, Shiva's face and upper body was clearly visible! The frontal photograph, of the shrine was also overshadowed by another large image of Shiva, which was superimposed behind - yet in front, of the altar. It looked like an etheric photograph because the palms, and artefacts, could be seen in front of, and behind, Shiva's image. The other two photographs of the shrine were also superimposed with Shiva's image! The four Photographs of his children on stage at the Christmas pantomime show had the same Shiva image on them, but just above the top curtain line, on the right hand side of the stage! Kiran took the photographs back to the developers for an explanation, but they could not give one. They pointed out that the photograph of Shiva on the Altar, was much smaller than Shiva's image, that overshadowed all the other Photographs.

It seemed that the 24 hour devotional gathering at Vas and Bharti Patel's house held deep meaning for Swami, and the over shadowed photographs were acknowledgments of the work that the Sai group did, and for those that had participated in the celebration of Swami's birthday.

Chapter 6

G O D

CREATION and En-soulment of Earth

A clarion call rang-out throughout the universes - we had been expecting it, for we were one-mind with the Elohim, picking up universal mind. We were to meet in the council chambers of the most high love and wisdom, to discuss a new plan that would unfold within a universe. The Elohim had envisioned raising the consciousness of life-forms in a manifest realm, on a planet called EARTH.

We met in a vast ovoid of light - an amphitheater of light, as pure spirit, reuniting with our brothers, and sisters, from other universes, for indeed we had never forgotten them. It was a joyous time as we assembled with others of our group, sharing our news, and creations, with them. Much beauty had been created as we spoke of our worlds, of water, and of the creatures within the waters. We became one mind with them, seeing their thoughts and the life forms on their planets; trees, rivers, mountains and forests. Some had intelligent life forms on them, side by side with purely animalistic and bestial species, but none of the forms were self-consciousness. Some of the groups came from galaxies in the furthermost corners of our vast universe, yet we were of one mind with them and the creators plan to raise the consciousness of all life forms, towards individualism on a chosen planet.

A hush came over all of us as we looked down to the centre of the amphitheatre; three beings of incredible brightness, were blending their colours and vibrations - it was beautiful to watch, then they merged, as one. Archangel Michael - the lord of our Christ office, Lord Metraton and Melchizadek addressed us. They were of the Avatar soul group, and over immeasurable eons of time had learnt to manifest physical bodies on many planets, without shattering the ethers, or destroying the life forms, on them. We had not yet learned how to do this, but remembered a little of the principle from let there be light, when Kolob had changed from a spiritual sun, into an etheric sun, to finally became a physical sun.

They greeted us warmly; Welcome brothers, and sisters of light. Was it not only yesterday that we created the universes, galaxies, and planes. We have seen your worlds, and creations - indeed we have visited with some of you, and they are beautiful indeed. They told us that the supreme creator assisted us in some of our thought forms; we knew this to be true for we were one mind within ITS essence, emanating from the etheric vortex of Kolob. We knew that thought forms from this centre, went out to all the universes. They continued; We were sent to this tiny planet, and received permission from its lord – Sanat Kumar, to carry out the creators wish. Therefore it is our responsibility to help these kingdoms to evolve… to raise their consciousness to individual awareness.

The creator wished us to evolve with all the kingdoms, as an experiment in creation. Free will and choice would be ours to use in whatever actions we undertook, provided that it was done in unconditional love and a non-willful evolutionary process.

When and if we had achieved our goals, we would take our knowledge to the furthest reaches of all the universes, and raise the consciousness of all forms, on them. They continued; Do you realize that if this experiment works, you will be the first beings within all the universes, to have immersed their consciousness in a low vibrational physical form, and hopefully be totally conscious of your godhood? You will work with the Devas in their realms, and be subject to their rules. Even though they will see you as god, it will not be easy, for earth is a low vibrational planet.

Michael, Metraton, and Melchizadek stood aside, as seven beings rose up from the centre of the auditorium cradling a beautiful planet, which we knew to be Earth. It revolved slowly before us in hues of green, blue, brown, and the yellow/white, of the deserts. There were snow-capped mountains, rivers, seas, and lakes which stood out clearly, it was indeed beautiful. They told us that this planet was part of a solar system in our universe, and that Sanat Kumar - the lord of earth, had moved 'its' consciousness from earth to the sun, to become the solar logos, in preparation for the experiment.

In the late 1960's, Ra-ab Houtep gave the group an insight into Sanat Kumar's en-soulment of earth, in its gaseous state, billions of years before; *A* ***great being was ready to en-soul this planet of yours, he was so filled with joy, excitement, love, and radiance, that gladly did his consciousness encompass this sphere in the universe. This great being entered his consciousness in your gaseous revolving mass, to solidify it. In so doing he created for himself an outer crust body, and then from the sheer exuberance of his joy, and vitality, he began to delicately touch the valleys, the grass, and lilies, and the most beautiful of flowers, and herbs. He touched the mountaintops with strength, power, and majesty, and the hillsides with forests, and streams. All creation - the insects, animals, and man, did he touch with his pen, and pencil. With great exuberance, and joy, did he en-soul his planet, giving to it - every aspect of it, all of himself, and all of his being in deep and wondrous love. He sank into his planet his very imagination, and his being-ness.***

We were told that we would have to learn how to enter our consciousness into its life forms gradually; we would use a tiny part of our vast celestial bodies of light to form a sheath body that would not damage the ethers or the life forms. The sheath body would be comprised of; an Astral, Etheric, Emotional, and Mental body, which would become known as the SOUL. They explained that this new sheath body might temporarily separate us from our pure spiritual body of light, once we moved our consciousness into the life forms. Therefore the experiment of Earth may present difficulties for some of us. They said it may make us forget our divine origins, and even our brothers and sisters of light.

We were in disbelief, knowing that it wasn't possible, how could we forget our soul groups, and oneness with each other? They smiled at us, with much love, and understanding and said, we shall see, but remember, we will be with you always. Remember also that some of your soul group will remain behind to watch over you, to guide, and impress you, to love and honour you. We shall meet soon to make final plans. About 2 billion years ago, earth had 'formed' to the stage that crude life forms began to evolve in the waters. A billion years later, Sanat Kumar released his thought-forms into the ethers surrounding Earth, and the Devic kingdoms would do the bidding of god.

About 18 million years ago, two vast etheric Sun discs - miniature worlds from another universe, approached one of seven outer arms of a galaxy, which would become known as the Milky-way. Commander Lucifer was the leader of one craft - the scientific aspect of en-soulment, and Commander Melchizedek of the Yahweh craft - the spiritual aspect of en-soulment. We came to earth as Lucifarian spiritual en-codement, from a far corner of our universe.

In a communication dated 3/3/1984, Tauung explained it this way; ***Whilst your solar system was in the process of banging itself into existence, cosmic scientists were busy collating material that would be placed in a space craft of gigantic proportions. You might say the select brains of the company, were brought to bear to make this machine. Behind all of this, the supreme creator's vision and desire brought this blueprint into being. We are now talking about the universe of Michael - your universe.***

There was an inner guiding council whose desire was to ensure that whatever en-souled into matter, would do so in perfect harmony, it was an inter-galactic council. This council had a spiritual leader, and a temporal leader.(Yahweh and Lucifer)

Michael could be described as the universal father of creation, on the outer planes, but behind him, is the spirit of the creator father/mother. Two colossal craft set out to seed your solar system,... the Bai'nor were responsible for guiding the other craft which was in the hands of great advanced scientists.

The BAI'NOR are the sons of god, who work directly under the auspices of the Elohim, They are highly evolved spiritual/scientific entities, that take 'seed thoughts' to new impulses of let there be light, to planets in unfolding universes. Their etheric craft are vast miniature worlds, scientific laboratories, mother ships, sun discs, etc, that can move at the speed of thought. These craft comprised the consciousness of many entities, using their Merkabah vehicles.

After millions of years acclimatizing to Earth's energy, and watching the species on it evolve, a meeting was called. Captain Lucifer - of the scientific craft, wished to move nearer to Earth, so as to speed up the evolutionary process of the species on it, from the outside, so to speak. This was not what we agreed to at the onset of the experiment, so we reminded him that it was agreed that we would have our being-ness in the evolving Ape/man species on earth, but he would not listen. Lucifer - a great lord of light in his own right knew of the potential dangers to his scientists, if they became trapped in the earth's forms. His manipulative, outside interference, would be contrary to the creator's original plans.

We tried to convince him, pointing out that the supreme creator clearly expressed that divine law must apply in the evolutionary process - in that we were to help raise the consciousness of the kingdoms of earth by en-souling the forms, and not by enforcing our will on them, from the outside. Melchizadek also pointed out that Lucifer's craft might damage the solar system - or at the very least, interfere with the vibration, and thereby harm the life forms on Earth, or even the very sun itself, because these craft were vast electromagnetic fields of power, and energy.

Sadly Lucifer had his own agenda, and was not prepared to make the sacrifice of incarnating his scientist's consciousness into matter. Lucifer brought his craft nearer to Earth.... the etheric sheath of his craft was encapsulated by our solar system, and transmuted into a physical/etheric form, thereby becoming subject to the physical laws of a solar system. The gravitational force of a large planet drew his craft nearer. Both the craft, and the planet, were destroyed. (Probably the mythical planet called Vulcan) Our universal astral bodies and Merkabah vehicles became separated from the cosmos, and we became trapped in a physical solar system. The ethers were also damaged which resulted in our sun developing a wobble.

The remnants of this craft and Vulcan are visible today as the rings of Saturn and the asteroid belt between Mars and Jupiter. Some of Lucifer's 'crew' realized their errors choosing to rethink the experiment of earth and eventually joined up with Melchizadek on Jupiter to continue with the creator's original plan.

Tauung, gave this communication on the 28/2/85;***These souls were deprived of the very basics of existence. It has been suggested to you that these souls were sent to Earth, which was the planet that had been seeded for them to carry out the experiment, but there were in between stages. It was my task to bring the company of this space craft to Jupiter; the staff and crew of the space craft were many in number. Opinion was divided as to where they should go, and what they should do, so some decided not to move with the main body. Tauung apologizes for covering old ground.***

It is from this point of view – rather than the scientific one, that Tauung desires to speak. The object of bringing them to the planet of Jupiter was to enable them to become familiarized once again, with a planetary body so that they could create for themselves a new creative mind vehicle. They had to learn once again to build for themselves a mind sheath body which took several millions of your years to do. They were no longer equipped to be able to move throughout the universe.

Some of his scientists remained with him, and made their Solar base on Saturn, and others made their galactic headquarters in Alpha Draconis, from whence they still interfere with earth's evolution. I have often wondered if Saturn is a word play on the word Satan?

This incident would become known as 'THE HITCH', because it was a set-back for the experiment of earth. Because of these events some Lucifarians - some of us, decided to begin the experiment prematurely. We moved into the planetary ethers, and developed a crude etheric sheath body which enabled us to co-exist with earths forms. About 8 million years ago, some of us decided to embody the evolving ape forms, in order to enlighten them. Most of us became trapped in these form bodies immediately; the low vibration of Earth and the animalistic mind of evolving ape forms, made us forget our divine origins completely. Whilst this was happening, Melchizadek moved his craft to Procyon, where it is to this day.

Ra Na Ta spoke of these times in a communication on the 10/3/83. I have only taken a few extracts of his message; ***Greetings and blessings, and welcome once again. When last we spoke, we told you we had brought our great craft to Jupiter, and from*** *there we embarked on seven different craft, nearer to your earth. You will remember that we approached earth with mixed feelings... we all had different reactions to the pull of attraction which this planet had on us. Some of us were more strongly drawn to it, so we moved our craft away.*

Seed thoughts - from the moon, were already established on your planet at that time, it but awaited the next step, which was to accept galactic beings to come to the moon with the sole purpose of bringing to earth the next stage of creation - conscious intelligent life. At that time we were sharply divided into two camps, but we did agree that our next step was to en-soul the planet, but could not agree how it should be done. We sent messages back to Jupiter who were in touch with the galactic government of this part of the universe, and knew of the blueprint plan for earth.

Most of us preferred to work with galactic law, despite the destruction of our craft - planet. The short cut was to move down and take possession of the planet, and experiment with our own free will. This was expressly forbidden by galactic law and the law of balance because earth had been en-souled by a great being - an over lord, and we were not permitted to usurp its authority. We met with the ancient of days – Sanat Kumara, to seek permission to make earth our home. Under his jurisdiction we agreed to develop his planet in co-ordination with the Christ office, and raise all forms of life back into spiritualisation, from whence it originated.

We formed a planetary hierarchy of senior members - consisting of ourselves, and were given the government of the planet. There were those who desired to enter in upon the material advancement of the planet, to take control of its natural evolutionary pattern, and speed-up that pattern. We knew that under divine law this could be done harmoniously in love. Some of us remained behind on the inner planes, and others went forth to manifest themselves - as etheric beings of light, in the physical.

About 4 million years ago the cosmic Christ sent his sons Sananda, and Avon (Jesus and John the Baptist) to our solar system in preparation for their involvement in the experiment. They visited the masters of the Mazzeroth star houses to familiarise themselves with their involvement in the plan. They immersed their consciousness with the solar logos - Sanat Kumar and the golden ones of Regulus, whilst viewing earth species from afar; the ape forms were slowly evolving as were other species, but all were at the mercy of natural earth movements, and cosmic energy rays.

3 million years ago, Sananda and Avon returned to our solar system with their father, the cosmic Christ. The cosmic Christ came from Kolob - the centre of all the universes, and was one of the seven Elohim. Later on he would take on many earth personalities, two of which were Krishna, and Sai Baba of Shirdi.

The cosmic Christ had its being-ness in the Mazzeroth house of Leo, working out of Regulus. Sananda, and Avon were slowly forming their sheath bodies in preparation for en-soulment of Earth, whilst observing its evolution. They knew that they would incarnate into a race of specially encoded people, who would become known as the 'royal family' or Judeans. Sananda and Avon moved nearer to earth, and had their being-ness with the solar logos, Sanat Kumar, to get a hands-on feel of the experiment. They were in touch with the brother-hood of light from Shamballa, the lords of the twelve star houses, the masters of the galaxy, the Christ office of Michael, the lords of the universes, and the Elohim.

An incredible message came through from JOHN THE BAPTIST, on the 16/1/1986 which Amy entitled, 'From paradise worlds'. A startling insight of the etheric star world, that Sananda and Avon came from; ***I must take you back beyond the stars, to give you a background of the beginnings. There were two of us.... you may call me John, a name that I have born on numerous occasions in various forms. We were a family group, and I had an older brother who always took the lead.*** (Sananda - Jesus) ***We belonged to a world of glory and magnificence, we still do. This world is beyond anything known to man.***

I followed my brother wherever he went, I still do, for he had trained me, you see. He was full of love, joy, and deep wisdom, and had always been, for as long as I can remember. We lived on a world that bordered the paradise world of Kolob belonging

to a group of evolving man, (spiritual man*) who had come up through the processes of the unfolding desires of the Elohim, in worlds of beauty, and spirit.*

From our world we could see seven stars across the skies, they were the temples of the consciousness, of the Elohim. Our father was a server of the light of the Elohim, in a great temple close to our star system. My brother sometimes served with my father, in the inner courts of the Elohim, and at times I was allowed to go with him. We formed a system of five planets - which you might call creation laboratories, each planet specialized in a certain energy pattern, which would be projected - in light, to the cosmos, forming specific creations, or worlds, with the power of the seven Elohim. Their scientists set out in their craft; we would watch them sail across the skies - beyond the horizons of vision, where they would meet another craft, much further out.

They would bring in their experimentations, and a new impulse of creation would burst forth into light. It was they who sent it towards a yet unformed galaxy, where it would precipitate into myriad solar systems. We saw brilliant flashes of colour across the skies, and knew that great ships had been sent forth into the unknown carrying a precious cargo of new life... We would watch a signal from the great temple of the Elohim, which encompassed the seven great planets, and see the great impulses of light going out….. and we would hear the stars sing in the sky. Our range of perceptions was greater than yours, for we could hear the stars sing together, as the glorious music of the spheres; music of all overtones, each one carrying a power impulse, from the creative desire of the Elohim….. This was what your scriptures spoke of when they said, 'the morning stars sang together, at the dawn of creation'.

The great star-ships went out across the heavens, towards a tiny galaxy, that had been discovered and coded for life. My brother and I were present with our father, when he received the commission from the Elohim, to speak the word let there be light, into your galaxy. We felt the thrill of it as one craft from our planet went into your galaxy, as part of a new creation, on a new world, in a new space of expanded time. We heard of the adventures experienced by that great expedition - but before that time, we knew that a new solar system had been discovered, on the fringes of a galaxy which would become another light midway station, for the expansion of light, into the voids.

We heard about your unstable solar system, the temporary hitch, and the plans for earth. A joyous occasion arose when my brother and I were called to our father and invited to leave with a star ship, to explore that solar system. It was John who packed the bags, preparing the way to go to the outer fringes with his brother, to see how the experiment was going. At the time we arrived, instability, and the resultant violent vibrations of the solar system, had increased, owing to a slight error, (The hitch)*which resulting in a change of plan. Earth was in the process of rising itself to self-consciousness through entities who en-souled it. These entities became trapped within the biosphere and the ionosphere - even the atmosphere of earth. A space commander from Metraton – under the direction of Michael and according to the plan of Melchizadek, sent stabilizing missions to the planet to enlighten them on their greater vision and why they became involved with Earth in the first place.*

My brother and I returned to our world disturbed.....the beauty of our home was magnificent when compared with our experiences in your isolated and threatened solar system... and we could not rest. My father sensed this and called us to him, he said, my sons I know that the harmony of your beings has been disturbed, and that there has become activated within you, that which was latent before - a desire prompted by love, and longing, to serve and re-harmonize. Do you still wish to undertake a mission to that solar system, and particularly earth? We had not yet formulated that desire, but became aware of it, when our father spoke.

It was required that we meet with, and learn from, the hierarchy of each of the mansion worlds of the lower heavens, (Our Zodiac star houses)*working from the fringes of the paradise*

worlds, in order that we might - in our consciousness, become the recipients of their unique energies and the divine plan of the father, in the lower heavens.

We undertook our training - and in so doing, came into contact - by awareness, with the opposing elements of light (Lucifer). ***We could do no other than adapt ourselves to the lower levels of consciousness, and would have to leave behind our paradise worlds and take upon ourselves denser bodies in order that we might effectively work upon the denser planes. It was a big decision to make and we could not have done so without it being presented to us as a commission from our father the ruler of the heavens... you might call him the Cosmic Christ.*** (Sathya Sai Baba) ***We sat in council with the Logi of the planetary hierarchy of the lower heavens, and were commissioned by your solar logos*** (Sanat Kumar) ***to go forwards - with his blessings, to bring salvation to man, and his earth.*** John's communication went backwards and forwards covering vast epochs of time, from three million years ago, to the onset of the experiment of earth.

A million years ago earth began to stabilize, in that movements of the earth's crust became less violent. Around 750 thousand years ago, various primate species, continued to evolve on earth. Earth's ozone was extremely dense; huge trees and vegetation, covered the whole surface, but despite this ape man were still able to survive. 500 thousand years ago, Earth's Ozone layer became more refined, but many species continued to be wiped-out by the unstable earth crust, and our solar systems periodic procession around the sun of Alcion, in the Pleiades, every 26 thousand years. Once again this would necessitate re-seeding of most species, and life forms.

Ra Na Ta continues with his wide sweep of Lucifarian man's involvement with earth at that time; ***We began our instruction to primitive man from the etheric worlds..... we walked and we talked with primitive man, and made him conscious of himself as a being. Prior to this time he was in complete harmony with all life on his planet; he was an individual, and perfect, following a normal evolutionary spiral of growth. Our task was to make***

him aware of his separateness from his source, and thereby accelerate his growth physically, mentally and spiritually.

In relationship to man of earth, we were godlike, and in that beautiful Eden we met with man; your scriptures tell you that man walked with god in the garden, at eventide. We began our instruction and warned man of the powers who was about to receive; in the process we must needs become involved with him. We were distinct from man- we sons of god, we were greater in stature. Our cranial development was elongated, denoting our spiritual advancement.... we were all knowing to man, and he began to worship us.

Adamic man - a highly evolved soul en-codement from another universe, watched earth's evolution from the ethers in preparation of their entry into the experiment. Those of us that stayed with the creators plan, continued to immerse our being-ness in the different species for brief periods of time; we found the nature kingdoms to be gentle - the trees and flowers especially, but became aware of heightened alertness, and fear, in the animal kingdoms, because of predation. We entered our consciousness, into the more refined Dolphins, and Whales - for short periods of time, to experience physicality, and movement; they were the earliest form of intelligent mammals to come to earth, and always survived traumatic earth adjustments, being highly sensitive to impending tectonic plate movements.

280 thousand years ago, THE SONS OF GOD, MARRIED THE DAUGHTER'S OF MAN. We breathed 'divine life' and consciousness, into the evolving man-ape forms, by en-souling them en-mass. Thousands of years would pass, but very few of us returned to the inner planes of enlightenment on death; we had no awareness of our I Am presence, and fled into an astral plane of illusion that we had established within the environs of earth, when the form we occupied, was no more.

On a visualization visit to Neptune, ORIEL gave this communication dated the 27/10/1983; ***The consciousness of man in other galaxies has come up through matter, but there was no sense of separation...... Your very advanced consciousness was obliged to descend into an embedded level of matter, having***

advanced for millennia of time on other star systems. Man's consciousness became cut off from his true spiritual being-ness, as he withdrew into matter, and had to learn once again, how to spiritualize matter.

For the first time you were able to express your free will in matter on earth, so you decided to plumb the depths, just to see how far you could go, and then you became embedded in it. Your consciousness descended far lower than that of the primitive life forms on earth, and that is why mankind is capable of bestiality, which the beasts were unaware of, or unfamiliar with.

In sinking his consciousness into matter, and using his free will to express the baser instincts of an energy that he did not understand, and could not control, man indeed became lower than the Beasts, but in truth, he was greater than the angels. Man had once again to learn to evolve, but by that time he had thrown all the kingdoms of nature back upon themselves. Earth species began to prey upon one another, whereas before they had eaten of the herbs of the fields...... they became carnivorous, as did soul man.

The experiment of earth continued to regress, and many of us became trapped in the very physical structure of earth; we were seen as ghosts, or evil spirits, by indigenous man, who yet had 'the sight'. Further efforts by our scientific brothers, and sisters, on genetic mutations on our form bodies, etheric helixes, and physical DNA, were carried out, but many of us remained trapped in duality, and illusion.

Cosmic scientists changed the DNA of primitive man, in that the right lobe of the physical brain was opened up in the hope that this would release trapped Lucifarian soul man, from these forms. In truth we were interfering with the original plan of unconditional love, and non-interference, and would ultimately incur Karma because of it! These changes brought about heightened thinking, and awareness, in some of them; at that stage, ape/man became man/ape. As soul beings, we were more able to impress their thoughts, and increase their consciousness.

In interfering with mans DNA, we had broken the supreme creators wishes for the experiment of earth. We all erred in this respect, trying desperately to bring our brothers and sisters back to the fold. The creator's plan was that soul mind would raise the consciousness of form mind, by impressing it with our divine aspects -our I AM presence, in light, and love, but we had underestimated the 'beasts' mind.

PER HOR made this observation during one of his early communications; ***Yes, there have been experiments conducted from time to time, as we have told you. The resultant efforts regressed from the original plan. They did not follow the plan that was laid out for them -they jumped the gun so to speak, and because of this they were removed from Eden - the spiritual world, to the east of Eden, the physical world..... where the experiments continued.***

Homo sapiens - a thought form, was still in the ethers, for the time was not right for their entry into the earth experiment. We were beginning to understand more about earth's vibration, energy, and life forms. Trapped Luciferian souls continued to flee into the astral planes of illusion, when the form they occupied was no more. Thousands of years passed, as man/ape became more orientated towards a tribal group consciousness. This came about as a means to survival, because other life forms continually prayed on them. It seemed to us that the experiment of Earth was now ready to begin in earnest, as more and more of us continued to immerse our consciousness in the different earth forms, for brief periods. We were beginning to understand more about earth's vibration, energy, and life forms.

When we incarnated again, bright shining beings shouted to us from the mountain tops, reminding us who we really were, but we ran from them in fear, for were they not gods who wanted to punish us? These gods continued to visit us in the Astrals, but we would move away from them in fear, for they were too bright for our eyes to behold. There were now three astral planes, as some of us, were slowly evolving to a higher consciousness. Even though the third astral plane was only slightly light filled, it was still better than being in the first astral plane, which was pure evil and illusion.

About 100 thousand years ago a new form precipitated to Earth. This form had been in the ethers for millions of years, and now lived quietly in secluded groups, throughout earth. This form was taller, lighter skinned, less hairy, and stood erect; initially they lived off the vegetable kingdoms only, but they would still have to fight for survival, because some of the animal kingdoms, would prey on them. This new form had a larger brain capacity, and therefore would be more intelligent, and hopefully live in harmony, with most of the kingdoms. They were HOMO SAPIENS, a perfect thought form creation from the mind of 'god', towards evolution on earth

At that time, hunter-gatherers ranged far and wide to find food, so it was inevitable that we came into contact with them. At first they were frightened of us, and ran away, but eventually we learnt their ways, and befriended them, for we too had evolved to become less beastial. They were pure and innocent, and initially would not eat the meat that we offered them, but that changed later. They were instinctual but not animalistic - as we had been for thousands of years, but that was also to change.

We were to en-soul Homo sapiens during our next embodiments; we discovered that more and more of us returned to the higher Astral planes, because of their increased consciousness. Periodically the earth's crust would readjust itself, bringing great destruction and loss of life forms, so the brotherhood of light would re-seed the new-born earth. New root races came to earth, from far flung universes and galaxies, whilst other beings - of the Avatar soul group, continued to guide us.

About 75 thousand years ago, our brothers and sisters of light from the Pleiades, began interacting with us more regularly; sometimes in their craft, and sometimes by incarnating into our soul groups, to help us link with our, I AM consciousness. Their re-reconnection with earth, helped to speed up evolution, albeit very slowly. Despite our gradual evolution, many of us we were still playing the game of birth and death, returning to the astral planes, and then reincarnating again. The fourth and fifth astral planes were now in existence and more light-filled; a strong vibration of unity existed in these higher astrals, as more and more of us were drawn to them.

On the 9/2/89, NATHANIEL gave this communication about our return to the astral planes, between incarnations; ***It is possible for someone moving into the astral planes, to remain there for a long period of time, stagnating. One does not evolve upon the astral planes, you only exist upon them according to the level of your belief system. Because you have understanding, you might enter into a fairly comfortable level of the astral plane world; but you would take with you, a sense of dissatisfaction, because something inside you would know, that your mission is incomplete. You would feel impelled once again - against your desire, to enter into another incarnation in the world of man. Whatever desires you had in your last incarnation will determine the astral plane that you return to; if it was possessions and greed, that your last incarnation needed, then you will gravitate to the lower astral planes of desire.***

We continued to be drawn to earth in our soul groups from the higher astral planes, finding it easier to link with our soul consciousness and guardian angels whilst incarnate, but others were still stuck in survival mode, on the lower astral planes of illusion. Most of those entities continued to be under the influence of Lucifer, who still controlled these planes, and continued to impose his will on earth evolution.

Over thousands of years, Lucifer Scientists spoke to us as beings of light; sometimes they merged with us, to adjust our light bodies to a lower vibration, thereby making it easier for us to adapt to earths vibration. They removed more etheric helixes from our soul body, which in turn would alter our DNA and further isolate us from our divine origins! It seems that Lucifer realized he was losing the war in heaven, so once again imposed his will for total control of earth, and humanity on it. The war between light and dark would continue for many thousands of years on earth, and in heaven, with darkness seeking to overcome the light and visa-versa.

52,000 years ago earth entered the null zone of the Photon belt again; lands would rise and sink, as earth tectonic plates readjusted to pure photon light energy. Another ice age would begin, with possible changes to earth's magnetic poles. Earth would stay in the photon belt for one thousand years, during which everything would be in darkness. This had been happening for millennia, as our solar system traversed the Mazzeroth houses around the sun of Alcion - in the Pleiades, every 26,000 years.

The master teacher RAH (Ra ab Houtep) responded to a question from Amy, concerning the null zone, during a communication on the18/2/93; ***You must ask your questions.***

(Amy; Our brother in Bulawayo, sent us information about the Photon Belt. About the planet going into a null zone, and all the energies that are thrown out of balance, and that the human body being part of the planet, is taking this on.)***That is so..... You have been entering the null zone for some short while now. As you move towards the focal point of it – these energies came from Kolob, you will find even greater disturbances. You will find a tendency towards fragmentation happening in the world scene; individuals wanting to identify with race group, and tribal groups, and all this sort of thing. You will see more and more of this happening, in the world scene. Your news media will report only what happens in the world scene, for it is draconian, and belongs to yesterday.***

Great spiritual up-liftment, and enlightenment, is taking place. The very liquids of the earth - and the planet of man, are affected by these electric imbalances, with the resultant confusion. You are heading towards - let's call it, your Armageddon point. Those who have chosen to walk in the light, will be the leaders in the new dispensation.

To divine mind, our solar systems entry and exit from the photon belt, had been observed for millennia, and is seen as a natural cosmic phenomena, but humanity does not have inter dimensional sight, and have been unaware of it. Having said that, about 15 years ago scientists, and astronomers, spoke of a magnetic belt approaching earth, but were uncertain what the implications were?

Avon came through on the 28/9/94, to talk about the light beyond Jupiter -the Photon belt; ***In this time, we are linked closely with light channels like yourselves, as we view across the heavens the approach of this great light. What we are doing now - in the great house of Aquarius and in the surrounding sign houses, is building a wall - almost *a ring pass not,* which will***

strengthen the already existing ring pass not of your solar system.

The ring pass not is a spiritual one, belonging to your soul planes, not the physical planes. For some while light channels have been schooled upon the inner etheric and astral planes, to build for themselves stronger vehicles, to meet the times that are approaching very shortly. It is not the first time that an outside body has entered into the ring of a solar system, or even your solar system, it has happened before, and there have been repercussion. Then the solar system settled down, to fulfil the next part of the divine plan.

(Amy; Beloved one may I ask you please, concerning that beam of light. We were given right in the beginning that this light was put beyond Jupiter to protect the experiment of earth. Is this what it is? ***Yes. This is the outward manifestation of it, coming more closely as a power force - not merely a static light, because your experiment is reaching its climax, or has reached its climax. Don't attempt to judge by human standards whether you have succeeded or failed; it is an unfolding experience involving all of us, but there is no fear, for you have a consciousness that is immortal, and you are a being that is indestructible.***

Dates concerning earth's entry into and out of the photon belt, seem to vary between our tapes, and the original information from an entity who called himself Ahton. In trying to bring all the information together, it seems that there is a 70 year period when we come under the 'influence' of the photon belt, and thereafter 50 years are spent in the periphery, which is called the null zone.

The time factors in this chapter are approximations. Notwithstanding the difficulties that the channel may have in verbalising the telepathic message from the being communicating, some entities do not always give the same information when it comes to the timing of specific events. An entity communicating has great difficulty trying to put 'no time' into human mind time. Sometimes they give us an approximation of human mind time in relation to the position of earth in a specific Zodiac house that earth was being influenced by, when a subject was being discussed. They may also be able to give us a time guide by recalling earth's entry into - or out of the photon belt, which they usually refer to as dispensations. The reader should therefore use their discretion in trying to fix a time, against any information in this chapter.

(* An etheric force field of light. In this instance a hologram around our solar system, put there by the scientists of Sirius)

Chapter 7

THE AVATAR

Bulawayo 1998

I had become very close to Kalpenar Hari and her sons Hitesh and Jamal, they were just beautiful beings. I often called in at their house to join them in the Aarti ceremony - an honouring of Swami, and the light of our divine essence, which they did every evening. Hitesh and Jamal were part of the main Sai group, and often shared our attunements, and meditations, on Saturdays and Thursdays. The divine love that Swami embodied, shone from their eyes, and it was a great joy to be in their company. Kalpenar, Hitesh, and Jamal devoted all their spare time and effort, to feeding programs for the underprivileged, begging and borrowing whatever was needed for the Sai children's home in the Matopos national park.

Kim Wing joined our group in late 1997, and worked very closely with the Sai group; at that stage of my life I was receiving strong intuitive guidance from my I AM presence, about special meditations, or honouring, that I should be focalizing. I would often discuss these thoughts with Kim - sound her out so to speak, and ever enthusiastic, she would soon be making plans about them, or adding to them.

A month before Swami's 73rd birthday celebrations, our group again took part in a 24 hour devotional honouring of Swami, at the Sai Baba centre in Bulawayo, and our gathering of light group, were asked to participate. Kim, Joan, Wendy, and I sang hymns, and finished off with a guided meditation. About three weeks later - just before Swamis birthday, Kiran left a message for me concerning a new manifestation of vibhuuti, at Kalpenar's house. We phoned her arranging to go around at lunch time; as we walked into the house a strong smell of vibhuuti pervaded everything. Kalpenar was smiling happily, then she took my hand and guided me into the lounge; she said, 'Bob, Swami visited us last night while we were sleeping, look what he did'.

Like many Hindu households, a chair for Shiva was placed at the side of a small Altar. We walked into the lounge which was buzzing with energy, and yet it was very peaceful; part of the red carpet had changed colour, it was now Grey! I looked again in disbelief then realized it was VIBHUUTI! We were trying to take in what our eyes were beholding; a semicircle of vibhuuti, stood out starkly against the red carpet, around the Alter and Shiva's chair. Even more significant were two perfect red footprints, in front of the chair surrounded in grey vibhuuti! The chair armrests were also outlined in grey vibhuuti, where Swamis arms and hands had rested on it.

We knelt in reverence in front of the chair, and I again thanked Swami for his incarnation. The energy of love in the lounge was almost overwhelming; it was as if he was still in the lounge. I sat in a chair facing the manifestation, quietly allowing the scene to sink in. Kim and Kalpenar had gone to the kitchen to make tea so I took the opportunity to get a closer look at the Altar, and photographs of her family on the walls; all the artefacts on the Altar - and some family photographs, had small amounts of vibhuuti manifesting on them. I could not take my eyes from the small neat footprints in front of the chair.

Swami is just over five feet in height and his footprints were small, I didn't realize how small. Kalpenar brought tea and I said to her. 'You are blessed and also Hitesh and Jamal'. She said, 'Yes, we know Bob. I got such a surprise when I walked into the lounge and could not believe my eyes… and then I said to myself, Swami **you are** tricking me. I woke up the boys and we prayed in thanks for the honour that Swami had bestowed upon us'. I arranged to see her later when I would bring Joan around after work.

Joan and I arrived but Kalpenar was not home. Jamal met us and took Joan's hand leading her into the lounge. Joan was amazed as he narrated the unfolding events to her. The vibhuuti on the altar had increased markedly and family photographs throughout the house were now all finely covered with it. A photograph of Kelpenar's late husband and the boys that I had looked at in the morning was now completely covered - except for their faces! Whilst Jamal was making tea, Kalpenar and Hitesh arrived. We hugged and were invited to stay for the Aarti ceremony. Before leaving Jamal gave us some vibhuuti which he scraped into small sachets from the altar shelving. Joan and I discussed the honouring that Swami had bestowed upon the family and, like me, she was thrilled at Swami's footprints on the carpet; to think that he had actually manifested physically in their lounge, what a beautiful personal touch and honouring for the work they did in his name.

The Sai children's home was 32 miles outside of Bulawayo, on the outskirts of the beautiful Motobo national park, an area of huge granite rock outcrops, and natural beauty. The Sai committee and the Kristiansen's, had approached a local chieftain, securing 30 acres of tribal land, to build a home for children whose parents had died of Aids. Funding for phase-one of the home, had been received from a European agency, and building plans were near completion. Work had already been done on three rondavels (thatched round houses) and an open workshop with borehole. A few children had already been taken in, and local 'mothers' were hired to assist the Kristiansen's in running the complex. The Sai group spent many weekends working to build up the facilities, using their own company transport to take material on site, whilst our group collected blankets, clothing, books, and toys, for babies and children up to 10 years of age. We were often invited to spend the day with Bent and Beta at Emakandeni, (the name of the home) bringing our own food, and fresh milk for them, as electricity had not yet been connected.

Beta had become a regular member of our Saturday morning group, but owing to petrol shortages, and new children being brought in, she was not always able to come into Bulawayo. Bent Kristiansen worked tirelessly building up the complex in the early days, sinking a borehole, building a header tank, installing a generator and wiring, etc. He pressed on tirelessly, creating a new village with willing help from the Sai group, whilst Beta was busy organizing food, the laundry, and a vegetable garden. Her duties - as foster mother, were never ending, by providing homely comforts, love and support for some of the children who had lost their parents. It was very difficult for them, because they naturally grew attached to the children, but knew that in some instances, they would not see them grow into teenagers, because there was no money or drugs in Zimbabwe to fight AIDS.

The smallholding had massive granite kopjies around it, and smaller rocky outcrops, so the contractor clearly indicated that any blasting, during foundation work, would be an extra to the scheme; short of digging trial holes all over the property, there was no way of knowing where the underground rock would be. Three weeks prior to commencement of the first children's block, Beta woke up early and visited the children; she returned to their rondavel made coffee and sat quietly thinking about the chores for that day. A movement caught her eye; she looked up in disbelief and realised it was Swami, about 150 meters away. He was walking slowly between some trees and looking at the ground; she restrained herself from running to meet him. Eventually he stopped, and pointed to an area in front of him, and the next moment he was gone! The site for project one had been established!

Donations were now coming in from all over the world, and as the building work had started, Bent and Beta returned to Denmark for a short holiday, leaving the home in the care of a manager, and the Sai group, and taking one of their early orphaned children, with them. They returned with their youngest son - a polite young man of about 24 years of age, who I got to know quite well. He showed me a ring that Swami had manifested for him during one of the Kristiansen's early visits to Puttaparthi; it was a pearl that moved around freely within two bands of white gold, and the ring itself, was made of gold. He told me that his mother and Swami were talking, when suddenly Swami turned to him and said, 'You want me to make you something don't you?' Before I could answer, Swami blew in his hands and manifested the ring and then he put it on my finger saying, 'One day you will know what it symbolizes'. I asked him if he now knew what it symbolized; he smiled shyly and said no. He continued with his story, pointing out that before Swami manifested the ring, he had blessed them all with upraised open hands, and also manifested vibhuuti for all of those present. I asked him what he felt about his first meeting with Swami, he said 'He was very powerful…. no…. his energy and presence was very powerful, he was also friendly'.

In June 1999 we attended the official opening of the home, which now had 31 children, comprising Boy's and Girl's between one-and-a-half to twelve years of age. It was a lovely day as the children sang, and danced, to traditional tribal songs; afterwards they sang English, and Ndebele songs, about Swami. The Sai ladies did lunch, after which I played my guitar and sang hymns, followed by a short talk about Swami. The local governor, education officers, and tribal chiefs were at the opening. After lunch Bent, Beta, Joan and I walked down to the eastern boundary of the plot, where a small dry sandy river would one day be dammed providing water for the local community.

The Kristensen's were called back to the gathering for some reason, so Joan and I continued with our walk, along the riverbed quietly enjoying each-others company. We found a small granite cave and sat talking for a long time; Joan's husband had developed Parkinson's disease, so we did not have as much private time together, as we used to, except of course at her house on Tuesday mornings. Kim and I attended the regular Thursday evening gatherings at the Sai centre, and participated in many Hindu festivities. We held special attunements, and workshops, at my house during which we shared the latest tapes about the Avatar, with the Sai group.

Ra Ab Houtep came through on the 16/3/95, to give this message about the avatar, the photon belt, and ascension; ***As for me, I shall call upon god and the lord shall save me, so said your Psalmist…. Ra ab Houtep would like you to be a channel of light this evening. Those of us who speak to you from time to time, have said to you; you are preparing for a very great shift in consciousness upon your planet…… This might be your Satan being bound, for a thousand years, Yes?***

(Dr; Beloved one about the ever coming one, will that be perceived on the inner planes, or at that level of consciousness) ***You have been perceiving the ever coming one in your heart for many, many of your years. You have felt a love for him….. there are others who go through a whole life time without knowing or loving him, or even being aware of him. He has a***

special place for you in his heart, as you do for him. Sometimes you feel him so closely that you feel tears come with it.

(Amy asked an indistinct question about the photon belt) ***At the speed of which your earth is travelling through this galaxy of yours, it is scarcely one second on the clock of eternal time. Your solar system travels through your galaxy at something like, 70,000 miles an hour.... you knew that, didn't you?*** (No) ***Oh yes, so an hour ago you were 70,000 miles back there somewhere, and an hour from now, you will be 70,000 miles away. It means nothing.... it does not even register in the vastness of physical eternity, let alone spiritual, The great message at the moment is ascension; attune yourself with your divine unity..... your divine incarnate Avatar - your incarnate Akashic record..... I'm sure he wouldn't like that description, because it is so much less than what he is..... but it might give you some idea of what he is, in relation to the evolvement of earth.***

(Dr; Concerning Sai Baba and reading Dwaal Khuul, would you say he is the Avatar of synthesis?) ***Yes! In every sense, of that word. He synthesises all the great religions of the world, and in pointing to their essence he says, you are one!***

(Dr; Beloved one, how does our great Avatar differ from the ever coming one)***He is the ever coming one*** (An indistinct group discussion took place) ***Yes? Do not give it names, do not look at personalities. Individuals incarnate, go to visit your Sai Baba, and they say this is the ever coming one. They recognise that what is coming from the incarnate Avatar, as being everything that they have been taught and aspire to, in their religions. He is not a religious leader incarnate, but the incarnation of the essence, and through the human personality of that essence, he keeps on saying look to god, look to Sai; Sai Baba is not his name, it's his designation. just as in the same way that Jesus' designation was the Christ, and Gautama's designation was the Buddah, and so on. It is difficult to look upon Bagawan Sri Sathya Sai Baba and think that he is not an individual.***

(Amy; But as he always says 'As I am so are you also') ***That is what the great Avatars have always said down through the ages. You are now experiencing a universal presentation of god in this***

earth life - god incarnate, not only in India, but in this room. Now is the time to deliberately put aside divisions, but paradoxically, still return to the source of your origin. This is what the great Sai Baba is teaching; he says, don't leave your religions and go to another one, and certainly don't come to me, to find a religion. Go back to your religion, and hear what god has to say. The lord your god is one.

Zimbabwe was becoming a no win situation for young people, especially for non-black Zimbabweans, because of government directives that only black Zimbabweans should be considered for government, or local authority vacancies. Inflation was rampant, and local education qualifications were unacceptable to the outside world; adding to this, continuing petrol shortages, food queues, etc, forced many of the Sai group to leave the country. Hitesh went to America, and three others - from our regular Thursday evening meetings, also left for other parts of the world. It was sad to see them go.

In December 1999, I was guided to do a feminine honouring during the last full moon in December - the last full moon of the age of Pisces. The moon had often been referred to as a feminine energy and I had often felt that women had been made to take a back seat to men, during the past 3000 years. Because of this they had sometimes been used and abused, by the dominant male energy. I was not in denial that the reverse had also occurred, but was driven to try and make things right in some small way, so as to clear the energy of imbalance for our entry into the new age of Aquarius. I discussed my ideas with Joan, and Kim, then sat down to put our thoughts of the planned the event, on paper. The program and events unfolded clearly within me, and it seemed that I had been intuitively guided for many months, on what format the honouring should be.

The gathering took place on the last full moon of the age of Pisces, which fell on the 23rd of December 1999. It had been a stormy afternoon, and was fairly cloudy when the honouring ceremony started, at 5.30 pm. A simple Altar was set up by Kim and my-self on the side board. It comprised 10 candles and cards, for the different religions, and persuasions, for the women of; Islam, Hinduism, Christianity, Buddhism, Catholicism, Mormonism, other religions, other spiritual paths, Judaism, and one for all other women, of earth.

A large central candle on a white lace embroidered cloth, sprinkled with rose petals, and two vases of flowers, completed the Altar.

Kiran invited two Islamic friends, and Kalpenar attended with 9 other Hindu friends - some of whom were Sai Baba devotees. Our group comprised Joan, Thelma, Kim Celia, Maud, and my-self; there were also three other people who I did not know. I was not sure who invited them, or what belief they followed, except that one of them was a Jewish lady. Prior to the ceremony, prayers were said in Hindu, Islam, Judaism, and Christianity by those present. Joan lit the main candle, which represented unity, love, and light. We stood in a large semicircle, as I opened the honouring by selecting a card and lighting a candle, from the main candle flame saying; I light this candle for the women of Buddhism, and then standing in front of Maude I said. On behalf of man, I ask your forgiveness for any deed, action, or thought, perpetuated against the women of Buddhism……. Please accept this candle, as a token of unconditional love, and forgiveness. Maud responded I except your forgiveness, on behalf of the women of Buddhism.

A Muslim friend of Kiran came forward, selected a card, and after requesting forgiveness on behalf of the specific religion, handed the woman his candle. It was a sacred and meaningful ceremony, dignified and sincere. The sun had set half an hour earlier, and the candles held by all of us, were the only lights in the room. One of the Hindu ladies said 'Bob, the moon is rising'. Time had flown - it was twenty five minutes past six, so we all went out onto the veranda of my house which was built high above the landscape. The moon was rising behind small dark clouds, highlighting them in a golden ethereal radiance. Kiran put his arm around my shoulder and said, Swami was with us tonight, Bob. Some stood quietly whispering to each other, and others were in their own thoughts, as the moon eventually cleared the clouds at 6.50 pm. Some of the ladies went to put the snacks out, and make tea. I asked if anyone wanted the lights on, a unanimous No! was the response.

We sat in the lounge or on the veranda, talking quietly in little groups, candles blazing; everyone seemed reluctant to go home, but eventually around 9.45 pm, most had left. Joan and Kim were spending the night at my house, as my car was in a petrol queue. It had been arranged that Kim's husband, would be collecting us in the morning, and Joan's sister in law, was looking after her husband Rod. We sat talking, and sharing our thoughts, until nearly midnight, when I realized that Kim was looking tired; she hadn't been well for some time and went to bed. Joan and I had one more cup of tea, and also retired.

Herewith a transcript by Ra Ab Houtep, entitled Avatars. It is dated the 24/12/95; ***Greetings beloved channel. Ra Ab Houtep would like to talk about the origins - if you wish, of your holy night..... origins might not be the correct word, but so far as your earth is concerned, it's the conscious entry of the Christ - the Christos, the Avatar spirit, pre-history, as far as you are concerned. The great civilizations which existed prior to the time which you refer to as Lemuria, and Atlantis, were preparing the vehicles of man to consolidate - so to speak, in physical form, the plan of god, the one god. After the subsidence of the last great dispensation of Atlantis, the world was divided into separate units,*** (lands/countries) ***because of geological upheavals, and various other reasons.***

Prior to the birth of an Avatar, a great feminine initiate would enter her consciousness - her soul being, into these communities, on your planet. She would bring forth an immaculate conception - a virginal birth, in a sense that she did not know a husband, prior to that birth. She sent forth a facet into human form that would be the receptacle for the Christ consciousness, entering into a form. The first known to man, was of course Rama, and it is to Rama that you actually owe your term, holy night; all his work began at the winter solstice - as it was known then, on holy night. He was conceived and born an infant, on holy night, and his incarnation - as such, goes back beyond your historic times; there is no historical record, but so great was the impact of this Avatar Christ soul on the planet through the land of India, that his memory came down in myth, and legend.

Then the time came for the advanced race of the peoples living in India, to receive a new impulse, because the energy of Rama was beginning to diffuse. It enabled other great souls to

incarnate in other lands. Then came Krishna, who is more or less historical..... but even that is open to questions, because he was the divine Avatar who came to change the whole course of human history. Spiritually he too was immaculately conceived on the holy night; his foster parents had taken him away from his surrounding circumstances, in order that he might bring in the new Avatar light. He was also worshipped in a stable, but cows were the beings - let us say, who represented Krishna. From that point onwards the cow was considered to be sacred in India, and it goes through to your times even now.

And so it went on, and shortly after his incarnation, the holy feminine initiate - Isis of Egypt, was immaculately conceived, and bore the child Horus, who was also an incarnate Avatar. Then we come into known history in a sense, because that history was inscribed on many temple walls, in a language which was even foreign to the Egyptians, of five to seven thousand years ago; the language is there in stone, and can be read. Horus also came to birth on holy night.... and gradually more of the Avatar soul group incarnated, into slowly developing races, around your planet.

The next land, that was ready for a divine incarnation, were the Persians. The Persians had an effect, and still have an effect, on your Muslim world these days, your middle east. Mithras was conceived immaculately of a virgin on holy night. Then Sibele - of the Greeks, also produced a child on holy night, who was worshiped in underground temples, in those days. The greatest of all feminine Avatars to incarnate - and she was an Avatar, was Mary of Bethlehem, who brought forth the universal Christ, the first practical known and experienced, Avatar. He gave during his life the message for all time and beyond it; she conceived this Avatar soul, and brought about the holy night, that you celebrate now.

Since then - the Christ soul, the Avatar Sathya Sai Baba, has once again incarnated, but into an entirely new dispensation, which is no longer confined, to any one corner of the globe; although it is of course, from the mother land of all religions, India. His incarnation, come forth from the soil of spiritual salvation, that had been cultivated in that holy land, for centuries, and centuries, and ages of time.

So today, the lord Krishna, the lord Rama, the lord Mithras, Horus, and Christ Jesus, are incarnate once again in your holy incarnate Avatar, Sathya Sai Baba. So this is the significance of holy a night; it releases into the world, the tremendous power of love, peace on earth, and goodwill to all men. This Avatar is the combined choral song of the universe, the Angel, the Archangels, and all the company of heaven. As channels of light, induct this into your world at this time, let this be a true and indeed holy period, for you, as a channel of the light. Let it flow through you, let it blaze out into your world, as you honour the mother of all avatars, the mother particularly of, Jesus.

She was of them all, the Avatar of Avatars, the feminine the holy principal, incarnate throughout the ages. She taught her son, all that she knew, and all she had experienced, from the early days, when the earth was in mist and shadow. She brought the golden thread of light and truth, from the celestial heavens of all glory, and offered the gift, into the hands of man; the gift of her son, his life and message, this is why you give gifts, because of the gift of the holy mother Mary, to the world.

In this time, a great, wonderful, and strong power of love peace and goodwill is emanating from the abode of goodwill and peace - Presanthi Nilayam, (Swami's home in southern India) *into all the world of man, through your incarnate Avatar, Swami… Sai Baba. So it is a significant time for all the Avatars are consummated in power for man and that in it-self, is a tremendous gift for humanity. Blessings and greetings, beloved ones… beloved channel.*

Chapter 8

GOD

On emerging from the photon belt 51,000 years ago, large islands had formed within a vast ocean of what is now called the Pacific and would become known as Lemuria. They were verdant with vegetation and comprised of mountains, lowlands, rivers, and lakes. These large islands had been pushed further out of the sea during the previous Photon belt entry, and were a tropical paradise.

Some forms had survived the earth adjustments on these islands, and elsewhere on earth, despite this dispensation beginning with a long ice age, which eventually receded 800 years later. Humanity thrived on Lemuria, as creator lords, and Avatars, walked amongst the population, from star systems unknown. A new culture was established on Lemuria, based on the Creators principle of love and light. Communication was often by thought, and in this way they linked with the other light centres, on earth. The Lemurians were taught the ancient mystery teachings unhindered, knowing that death was an illusion, and that they were in truth eternal, immortal, and indestructible beings of light; they loved and honoured the nature kingdoms, and knew how to communicate with the Devas. They rarely ate meat, preferring fish, and fowl, which they thanked and blessed, in ritual sacrifice.

Being a large island population, and technologically very advanced, they understood the ocean currents and winds, and made boats that took them far and wide, to the Polynesian islands, and the west coast of North America. They could see beyond the veil, and prospered in a society of love, and respect for one another. They learnt the power of crystals, and how to communicate with the cosmos through them; they also programmed crystals to heal, having asked the mineral kingdom Deva, to help them.

Many Lemurians lived for hundreds of years, and when some of them were ready to 'go home', they simply lay down near their graves gently breathing in their last breath, and merging with the eternal flame of their higher selves; sometimes there was sadness, but also incredible joy in the community, for they knew where their loved ones would be going. Others were taught the law of transmutation and ascended with their bodies, but amongst them still were many who lived at human mind level only, and would need many future incarnations to equate their Karma, and fully understand their divinity. Some Lemurians left earth en-mass, returning to their home base - the Pleiades. A hundred and forty four thousand would remain with Earth, setting up etheric spiritual centres - one of them at Mt Shasta. There were now five astral planes, and those Lemurians who had not ascended, moved into this plane which was also called the 'Summer lands'.

On the 23/1/86, John gave this fascinating communication about his and Jesus' activities prior to this time period; ***When John and his brother*** (Sananda/Jesus) ***had familiarized themselves with the lower heavens – the Mazzeroth, that part of your galaxy which effects your solar system, they became familiar with denser bodies of consciousness, and met with the solar logos - the Christ of your solar system.*** (Sanat Kumar) ***The body that John talks of is the Merkabah/Shakinah light body. Our mission was to be vortexes of love and light, under the auspices of the solar logos. At the time that John talks of, there were yet no form bodies on your planet.*** (Physical man forms) ***It is difficult for John to talk of time, space and consciousness...... I find myself going backwards and forwards in time, in this communication.***

Whilst we were with the solar logos, we watched the unfolding events on your earth. Beings would come to your earth and attempt to stabilize it, and later on, as man came up in evolution, he played his part in stabilizing it. A time arrived when the experiment of evolving man on the planet, had reached a higher level of intelligence, so my brother and myself, came down, taking on even denser sheath bodies. We entered into the being – the planetary logos, and knew at that time, that we would not be released back to our homes, until our earth

mission was completed. Our mission was very simple; to bring the purity of the love, and light, of the father, into living manifestation on earth; we would do this with the lords of light, who represented the Elohim, in all of the kingdoms.

We learnt to work with the higher angelic kingdoms, as well as the lower Devic kingdoms - and in identifying with them, we took on even denser bodies. These bodies were not visible to the human eyes of incarnate man, but the Devic lords, and their workers, could see them. We met advanced souls who had their being on the higher astral plane; they had incarnate experience, and were on their way up to the governing council of the planet. (Shamballa)

Forty thousand years ago - Adamic man.

Just before the end of the Lemurian dispensation - about 40,000 years ago, a great event occurred. **Adamic soul man,** incarnated into man of earth, having been in the ethers for nearly two million years - or the blink of an eye! Adamic Man, came to our solar system from another universe. They were a new en-codement - a new blueprint soul group that could not easily be manipulated by the dark lords, as had been happening for eons. The goal of the gods was that Adamic man would become **Adam Kodman – Ascended man,** and the metaphorical story of Adam and Eve, would be told but never fully understood.

25,000 years ago the 1st Atlantian dispensation began, as earth emerged from the photon belt. Luciferian and Adamic souls spread far and wide across the face of earth. Our choice to incarnate within our original soul groups was still important to us, and spread across many lands with different cultures. In-between incarnations, we met in the higher astrals, planning our next embodyments. Some of us were beginning to understand, that we were human BEINGS, and not just being HUMAN.

The powers of darkness continued to try and enslave the minds of humanity, where some of our brothers and sisters of light had not evolved to a knowing-ness, that they were more than their human bodies. Many of us continued to play the game of life and death, returning to the lower astrals of elusion in shame and confusion. Gods still visited earth, shouting to us from the mountain tops; some of us had an affinity with them, somehow knowing they were telling the truth, and that we were indeed one with them. We saw their craft in the skies, but also the craft of the powers of darkness, and sometimes we were not sure who was who.

We often re-incarnated to test each other during embodiments to equate Karma, and some began to understand that death was an illusion, and that we were in truth eternal, immortal, and indestructible beings of light. Our tests or agreements prior to incarnation were very severe - from a human minds viewpoint; murder, rape, and physical abuse were often agreed to, between two incarnating souls for Karmic reasons. Our guardian angels and discarnate soul group, would stand by in the hope that they would be able to impress upon us that what we were undergoing in that life experience was agreed to, and an illusion to our pure spiritual being-ness.

At this juncture I will share with the reader part of communication from the Master Jesus that came through on the 13/1/87. At that time, he had only recently started communicating with the group; Jesus was responding to chapter 110 of the Aquarian Gospel, being read to the group by Amy; ***Please do not feel any strain or pressure, after all you are not in a schoolroom, and we have an absence of schoolmarms, and masters.***

(Amy; Beloved one, you spoke of Mary of Magdala. We have difficulty in understanding morality; how do you explain earth morality, against that of Mary Magdalene?) ***Sometimes a soul may undergo the most ghastly of experiences –in so far as the world of incarnate man is concerned, because it knows it needs to experience all the vibration, in the form world of matter. The soul knows what is God-like, and what is not God-like, but the incarnate soul must strive to find the meaning of the two. Where one - who is incarnate, has harmed the spiritual progress of another in the earth life, then that transgresses spiritual law, but has nothing to do with man's morality.***

Behind man's moral laws, lies the spirit of experience, and also the experience of the laws of cause, and effect (Karma).

What may appear to be a great crime against someone, might be an equating of experience; it might be that the one initiating the crime, and the one receiving it, are in complete accord, although it may not appear to be so.

About 18,000 years ago - in the age of Libra, the second Atlantian dispensation ended, as large areas of land sank beneath the seas. Earths tectonic plates buckled, between Africa and Europe, causing massive earthquakes and volcanic eruptions. This affected lands in our present day Mediterranean area, specifically southern Italy, Greece, Turkey, and the North African continent encompassing some of present day Egypt. During these movements, parts of Egypt rose from the sea bed, including the lion of Regulus, which had been under water for 1000's of years. The lion of Regulus would eventually be re-sculptured, as the Sphinx. The Nile had also changed its course, and now ran from South to North. Advanced Lucifarian and Adamic initiates of the light knew of the impending subsidence of Atlantis, and moved to different lands, Mesopotamia, the misty isles, and Egypt being the main ones.

Ra ab Houtep, gave an overview of events up to this stage of my story, which goes back at least 300,000 years. It was dated, 9/3/78 and entitled Sons and daughters of God; ***There was a time many, many thousands of years ago when you understood more than you do now. A great civilization terminated its progress, and almost terminated the world with it. You refer to that time as the era or epoch of *Atlantis*. Let Ra Ab Houtep endeavour to stir a memory in you. We were there together, my sisters and brother*** (The Arel group). ***It was a time when mankind had developed his mental powers to a far greater degree than they have today, but the mind and emotional body of man became rebellious, and brought about the destruction of all form in that civilization.***

At the time when the civilization of Atlantis terminated in violence and upheaval the poles shifted and earth turned in another direction, there were those who had for knowledge of what would take place, brilliant men and women - scientists. They built for themselves great flying laboratories....... you have heard of the story of Noah and the ark.

So the sons and daughters of god came to earth, and the remnants of primitive man saw them, and then they transmuted their craft and themselves and lived side by side with primitive man. The sons and daughters of god were able to raise the consciousness of the sons and daughters of primitive man; there arose amongst the sons of a man, souls who cried out to the gods to become equal with them, and they were taken to the temples of learning, which were built by god.

*There came a time when the sons of god 'married' the daughters of man..... and children were born who were half man, and angel. And then Ra Ab Houtep was born to a daughter of man, and because he was born from a son of god, he was initiated into the temple rights of ancient Egypt, *before your history begins - as you know it*. Because Ra Ab Houtep was a son of god, he was able to be a bridge between man and god. The temple priests had powers and implements of which you have no knowledge yet to this day; not by the sweat of his brow did he earn his living...... but through the power of his mind to visualize and create for himself, what he needed - and what those around him needed.*

By the power of thought, he was able to take massive stones and transport them over incredible distances to build his temples and his pyramids; indeed these great blocks of stone sailed down the Nile in reed boats, but the power that was sent into them made them as light as feathers. You my children knew of these things, but you did not wield those powers

(Amy; Beloved one, were there instances of death between the sons of god, and the daughters of man in those days?) ***The sons and daughters of god did not die - as you conceive of the word, their physical bodies did not carry disease or disintegrate, they had passed that point; they learnt how to transmute the atoms of it, into finer etheric substance. It was not their mission to become involved in materiality that is why not all of the sons married the daughters of man; those that did, did so at tremendous sacrifice and love, which bonded them to the planet for thousands of years. There are some of them who still float as light as feathers***

around your planet, and have been identified as beings in strange machines…… space craft.

(Dr; Before the sons of god married the daughters of man, did primitive man have consciousness?) ***Oh indeed they had self-consciousness, but it was so buried in their body consciousness, that they might very well have been completely blind…. they were imprisoned in it. True self-consciousness, is the recognition of one's own being with that of the universal divine.***

(Amy; Beloved one what colour was their skin?) ***I expected you to ask that question. Primitive man was darker skinned, with much hair on the body as well, but when the illumination of the mind began to take place, so did the body become lighter skinned, and less hairy. If you wish to ask Ra Ab Houtep questions, please do, you might even wish to interrupt Ra Ab Houtep, if you wish.***

As time proceeded more and more of the sons and daughters of god left earth and moved out into the cosmos, leaving behind them all the vast and wonderful knowledge of their experience for those who followed, to take and build upon. It was foreseen that there would come a time when the awakened consciousness of the ordinary man would assert itself in the affairs of the earth, but because of their fear - their animalism, they thought in groups of one mind. Gradually the power was given to man him-self, because each man and woman has to learn to stand alone - with god, in full consciousness of being one with the creator.

13,000 years ago earth re-entered the photon belt, and 1000 years later emerged from it. Once again a third of earth was ice covered, and land masses had changed again, but not as much as in previous dispensations. It would be another 200 years before the ice fully receded towards the North and South poles, and vegetation covered these areas of earth. Much of the Yuga Empire (China area) had become inundated by the Sea, forming separate islands; the dark lodge had moved to that land in the previous dispensation and subsequently adopted the dragon as their emblem. Alpha Draconis and the Bear constellations were still the galactic head-quarters for the dark lords.

Once again, the Cetaceans had survived earth movements, for they had long ago learnt to read the signs, moving away from the tectonic plates when earth readjustments were eminent. They hold the total history of earth within their group soul consciousness, being the earliest form of mammal that manifested in the waters, and the longest to survive. The symbolic story of Noah's ark would unfold, but in truth, THE ARK was the re-seeding biospheres of light, containing all earth species that were destroyed, during earth's entry into the photon belt. Earth still lived with the nick-name that the Pleiadians had given us, 'The planet of angry gods'. Egypt and India would be the gathering points, for great teachers, some of whom would incarnate - or as Avatars, manifest physical bodies, to bring the ancient wisdom teachings to many different lands on earth, during the dispensation of Pisces.

11,500 years ago, the 'Golden Ones' from Regulus created a powerful vortex of light, near present day Cairo. This would become known as the city of light, or the city of the sun, but the early Egyptians called it the Temple of ON. The ancient wisdom teachings would go forth to the world of man from this centre, which was later re-named Heliopolis, by the Romans. Recent discoveries at On are raising eyebrows amongst Egyptologists at this time; It seems that they have discovered a canal that originally joined the Nile. I find this most interesting because on one of our tapes the master Jesus talks about his revisit to On, during his 40 days in the wilderness; he said that he sailed out from the city of On into the Nile river, which confirms these latest discoveries. The vortex of light at On flooded the land of Khaam and great initiate training was taught to the simple isolated tribes that lived in that land, and also the inner secrets of the ancient wisdom. I use the word simple in that they were peaceful, and content with their slow human evolutionary path, with few - if any, demands for worldly possessions. At soul level they were very advanced beings, who worked the land and fished the waters, but moving quietly among them, were great master teachers.

The pyramids at Saqqara and Giza would eventually be built with ancient cosmic instruments, one of them being the Ankh. The cosmic architect, Sousa, designed and supervised the building of them, which were duplicates of the great pyramids on Regulus. Thoth was the celestial mathematician who envisioned them, and understood the sacred geometrical calculus, behind them. The pyramids are powerful cosmic instruments linking us to our mazzaroth Zodiac houses; the capstone of the main pyramid will eventually be reunited with it, prior to ascension. It was removed for safe keeping, until such time as man woke up to his divine origins; our tapes say it was made of electrum, a mixture of gold and silver. Originally the pyramids were priesthood training temples - not tombs for the Pharaohs, as is popularly believed.

The early Egyptians did not use slave labour to fashion and heave the huge Granite blocks - some weighing hundreds of tons, from Aswan, to the Giza plateau about 500 miles away. They were indeed transported down the Nile by reed boats, but had been made weightless by Divine mind thought energy, and the Ankh. The Ankh and other ancient instruments were able to change the atoms within the stone columns, by transmutation. Only advanced initiates, working in unconditional love, and light, knew how to use them. Ultimately they would be hidden in sacred places throughout earth; some are buried under the sphinx, and others are kept in secret temples, in the Himalayas.

Specially trained initiates, from temples bordering Nubia in Egypt, would move throughout earth. Over the ensuing thousands of years - and under guidance of divine mind, they built the sacred temples of learning along the Nile. Some of these highly evolved beings, were of the 'ROYAL FAMILY'- a chosen race group that was later to become known as the Israelites. Early Egyptian initiates of light, continued to re-incarnate throughout earth, into other evolving races that were ready to receive the light of full awakening.

9,000 years ago the last Atlantian dispensation ended, as a third of the Greek, Italian, and Turkish mainland suffered cataclysmic earthquakes and volcanic eruptions, again. These lands sank beneath the waves, with little if any evidence of their existence today; the only visible remnants are the numerous small islands like Crete, etc. Some Atlantian initiates knew of the impending destruction, and moved to the promised-land, Egypt, and the misty isles before the event.

John continues with his communication of the 23/1/86; ***We met with Melchizadek, Enoch, and their councils. During the time***

that we were with your solar logos, we watched the cycles going around the great central sun of Kolob, and also the cycle of you solar system, going around the great houses of your lower heavens. (Around the sun of Alcion in the Pleiades) ***There were high periods of light, and then low periods of darkness. We became actively involved with physical man during the Piscean age, as the wheel of that cycle, had just about reached its bottom. John incarnated ahead of his brother, to prepare the way. It was John's task to counsel Enoch, Melchizadek, and Abraham; the bible has reference to the angel who spoke to Abraham….. do you wish to speak?***

(Dr; Beloved one, did not Melchizadek speak to Abraham?) ***Oh yes, and initiated him. The angel appeared to Abraham, and instructed him to go into the land of the Nile, with his wife Serai, so that he might learn of the wisdom that had been growing in that area, and Chaldea.***

(Amy; Beloved one, what body were you in at that time?***In a Shakinah body; the greater Merkabah vehicle, had become enshrouded in the Shakinah body, at that stage. John became isolated from his true home, and could only faintly remember his origins. We would incarnate physically into man's world, into bodies which were of a higher vibration than ordinary evolving mankind; they would therefore be superior, but were still man, and therefore identified with the physical body of man - as man, but they would be set apart.***

After the upheavals consequent upon the subsidence of Poside, (Atlantis) ***the holy royal family, were prepared for the next dispensation. In a high state of consciousness, they incarnated into the valley of the Nile. They came to remind mankind that they were sons and daughters of the pure light and to seek to identify with the pure light. This is the message that the holy family have always given to mankind because man could not understand the simplicity of it, so he created pantheons of gods, to identify himself with nature, by exulting Devic beings to angelic status, and indeed to divine rule. That is why conflicts have come in man's evolving, spiritual, consciousness.***

(Amy; Yes we understand, thank you beloved one.) ***John worked with the advanced ones of ancient Egypt….. as scribe and as architect. He came as priest king, with those that worked in the valley of the Nile; his purpose was to create a greater family, to choose and select, advanced beings, in man's world. At the great city of light - which you call ON, he established the celestial power that would dispense to the world the concept of one light…… you also call it Heliopolis, the city of the sun.***

(Amy; Beloved one, we are so privileged to converse with you, we can only say thank you my lord) ****John!*….. John! Are you not gods?***

(Amy; Beloved one the great master Thoth, is that one of your incarnations?) ***Yes, and also Im Houtep….. and also Moses.***

(Amy; Oh? How does Akhenaton stand with that?) ***Part of the same family. By the time of Moses, John was becoming familiar with a human form, for he too had brought his consciousness into human form, at that stage. His great mission was the law, which he equated with love, with god, and harmony. Then he had to create other laws to make the great law understood….. and then his followers created even more laws than that, until eventually, Moses became outlawed.*** (Divine humour)

During John's periods away from earth - back to the inner planes, he was able to enter into silent communion with his brother. We knew we were brothers, and also of our star sent origins. At the time of Elijah, and Isaiah, 'their' consciousness came into the sphere of the planet of man. . . At the time that he returned to give the law, his brother began to descend towards the earth of man.

As the time drew near for them to incarnate, they chose their disciples….. they met with their earth family on the inner planes, and began to plan for the descent of the Christ. John did not die within the human body until his final incarnation….. he always transmuted it. The bible tells you that Enoch was caught up into heaven, and Moses went up into the mountain, and was not seen again, and so was Elijah caught up and never seen again.

The reader may be confused as to why Avon refers to his different embodiments and incarnations as, He, John, or Im Houtep, but once again I must remind the reader that Avon looks back on those times and earth experiences in retrospect, because he cannot identify with an Earth personality that he took on, as being more important than his real divine being-ness.

3,600 years ago the last great Egyptian epoch ended, after the reign of Akhenaton. The Hyksos, Greeks, and other invading tribes, would sit on the throne as Pharaoh's from time to time, but throughout these periods of spiritual decline, secret desert temples, and the valley of the shrines, were always in touch with the pure priesthood in upper and lower Khaam. The fabled winged Pharaoh's were of the Avatar soul group, who would appear or disappear amongst their people at will. Their initiates would spend two nights and three days in a Pyramid sarcophagus, alone. This spiritual test/initiation was undertaken without light, food, or water; if they survived the ordeal, they would have gained total awareness that the physical form was merely a vehicle for the soul, which was eternal, immortal, and indestructible.

Akhenaton left earth in ascended consciousness, and was to be followed by an Avatar called Moses, who would be perfectly placed to lead the 'royal family' into their promised land. The Channels, and scribes, at that time, recorded the life of Moses, which would become the foundation of the old-testament book that would become known as the Bible. In other lands, the ancient wisdom teachings would slowly go into decline, as invading tribes - infiltrated by the dark lords, influenced the populace to revert to pagan, and nature worship. The future evolution of earth was handed over to the Brotherhood of light in Shamballa, in preparation for the indwelling of the light of truth, the Christ - Jesus.

Many of us continued to play the game of death, and re-incarnation, but on return to the astral we began to understand the reasons for our incarnate errors; in retrospect we remembered our reasons for incarnating the last time, always striving to get it right the next time. Some would succeed, and others - for karmic reasons, would have to incarnate again, and again, 'for as we had sown so would we reap'. The war of light verses dark continued on earth and in heaven leaving the supreme creators plan for earth in the balance.

The years passed as new enlightened civilizations rose, and sadly fell again, but the Summer lands - the 5th astral plane, and the 6th, and 7th mental plane's, were growing with new initiate souls. We met, discussed, and planned our next incarnations, but still chose to incarnate into our own soul group. Great teachers such as; Abraham, Alexandra of Macedonia, Homer, Plato, Cyrus, Lao Tsi, Aristotle, John, Krishna, Shiva, etc, anchored the light of truth, in different lands throughout earth. Some of them would incarnate into the ancient Druids, and Celtic tribes, of the misty Isle's, where they were given advanced knowledge of earth energies, the ancient wisdom teachings, and the Devic kingdoms. Sadly - as had happened in previous epochs, when these advanced teachers left, the pure truths would become adulterated, or forgotten, and the tribes would rely on myth, and legend, handed down from generation to generation.

Sananda, and Avon, would be known by many names in many lands, and in this last communication he acquainted us of a few of his many embodiments. Sananda would also have many 'Avatar manifestations' throughout earth, one of which was amongst the 'red' Indians, where he was known as White eagle. The royal family were drawn to incarnate into the nomadic Arab tribes in Canaan, Samuria, and Palestine. A time of great change was upon man, and woman of Earth, as Tauung - the lord of Virgo, appeared before Mary, using the name Gabriel, in preparation for the advent of Christ consciousness, entering fully into the earth envelope.

On the 16/2/86 John gave this insight into those times; ***John fulfilled all his training, and returned to the inner plane, to become acquainted with those who would be his Earth parents. John's parents - Zacharia and Elizabeth, were prepared through many lifetimes in Nasserite communities, and other communities of holiness, throughout the known world. In a previous but one incarnation, they had incarnated in the holy land of India, and prior to that, they had been incarnate in Israel, in the Essene community. In earth years they were almost passed their time of child bearing, when the stars in the heavens lined up in the right conjunction……. On the rays of*** *the inner planes of Kolob, John was able to bring his consciousness into the earth, and the body of Elizabeth.*

The Sanhedrin knew of Johns birth, and eventually would try to take the life of Zacharia...... but Zacharias and Elizabeth escaped to Egypt, where they learned of Elihu the teacher at On. Joseph and Maria lived in the hills of Galilee, towards Sumaria. When Jeshua entered his consciousness towards his mother, wide opened the heavens....... as you know, the commander himself (Archangel Gabriel) *came and spoke to both Elizabeth and Maria, bringing with them the energies of Kolob, in their great star ship.*

Some of your stories have said that when Maria visited her cousin Elizabeth, John leapt in the womb for sheer joy..... that is because, standing beside our parents to be, we realized that this was the fulfilment of our earth task. We clasped our hands, and embraced in brotherhood, as the embryos rejoiced. Whilst John was growing up, Jeshua was also growing up; they met on one or two occasions but did not fully know each other..... and yet they recognised the soul bond. John knew he was to be the fore runner of the Messiah. Jesus was not sure if he was to be the Messiah until his 30th year, but knew he was to be the saviour of mankind. When John met Jeshua on the banks of the Jordan, he heard the voice of the commander say, 'this is my beloved son, in whom I am well pleased'. John himself was not sure until the moment he walked towards me down the pathway; great aura of beauty, and peace, pervaded the very atmospheres.

The following communication from John, came through on the 8/4/86; a most important insight, into that incredible time, prior to, and after the birth of Jesus, an outstanding message! ***Shalom, blessings, thank you. It is alright if John gives you some stories?***(Yes please) ***His-stories.....you don't mind? I wish to create the climate that existed in man's world, at that time..... John apologizes if he jumps backwards, and forwards, and does not follow your chronology. Jesus perfected himself through many life times to become the channel through which the Christ would ultimately manifest itself. He belonged to an Avatar soul*** *group. From time to time, he who you know now as Jesus,*incarnated* into man's world - in different countries of the ancient world, to bring light. His was known by different names in those areas; he was of course the Christ Enoch, and the Christ Melchizedek, to name two of his great 'incarnations' of consciousness. In between times, his soul group also incarnated as teachers, and instructors, you do know that?*

(Amy; Not quite in that sense, beloved one?) *Yes, *you are astute*.John alone incarnated, of the two brothers. John always incarnated as a forerunner of the Avatar soul group and has also born many names, in different lands. Before his incarnation in Israel, he was the Hebrew prophet Elijah. John's brother brought his consciousness into matter from the paradise worlds where a body was prepared for him, the body of Jesus as you call him.*

Unlike John, he did not lose his contact with the paradise worlds, whereas John did. John had to become coarser and coarser, in order to be fully identified with the world of man. Light entered suddenly into the Hellenes, producing an explosion of genius beginning with your Homer, and Pythagoras, Alexandro, Socrates, Plato, and lastly Aristotle. The reason for these incarnations, was that the soul of man would become revealed to man...... Their purpose was to bring to birth in man, an awareness of a higher self and light...... great leaders like, Pericles, and Alexander of Macedonia, reaped the fruits of their fore-runners, bringing their genius to its highest.

From the time of the Maccabi's onwards - until that great day, the community of the Essenes, the secret and silent brotherhood, were preparing and watching the skies. Great heavenly companies ascended towards earth, at that time; the teacher of righteousness - John, had fulfilled all his training, and returned to the inner planes.

When the stars in the heavens lined up in the right conjunction's, and on the rays of the inner planes of Kolob, John was able to bring his consciousness down, into the body of Elizabeth. The birth was known to the priests of the temple in Jerusalem, and the Sanhedrin. Ultimately, Zacharias was murdered by them….. but Elizabeth escaped with John, as you know. They too went to Egypt, where they learnt of Elihu - the teacher, who prepared them. You know that our parents were obliged to flee into Egypt, to the glorious city of ON…… into the temple were Elihu - an Israelite, was the chief priest. Our parents were taught the ancient mysteries, for now that we had entered our consciousness into man, we needed the guidance, and instruction, of our parents. Then we returned to Galilee

(Amy; Beloved one about that journey, was it done in a craft?)

Yes it had to be, for in those times it was not advisable to expose the light to the evils of man's world; we literally arose, and went into Israel. On our return, Elizabeth, and John went into the hills of Judea, to be instructed by Mathenos - an ancient Israelite, well versed in the ancient mysteries of Khaam, where he had trained for this time. Mathenos taught John much, he was his spiritual father.

Even as a child, the masters of Israel would seek out John, for John knew the spirit of the law, which they did not know. As he grew older, there were those who sought him in the desert, for John was alone in those days. Mathino had been gathered to his fathers, and John laid him to rest in the deserts of Judea. Whilst John was growing up, Jesus was growing up also; they met once, or twice, but did not fully know one another, and yet they recognized the soul bond between them. John knew that he was to be the fore-runner of the Messiah….. but Jesus was not sure, except that he knew he was to be the saviour of mankind. At the time that John talks, the saviour and the Messiah were thought to be one people, belonging only to the Jews…… They talked about a man of sorrows, acquainted with grief, and about a risen messiah; it was given to some of the Sanhedrin, that the two were one, but they thought that he belonged only to the Jews, that is where the confusion lay in those times….. Even Jesus - until his 30th year, was not sure whether he was to be the Messiah of the Jews, or the Christ of mankind.

When Jesus met John at the river Jordan for baptism, the etheric heavens opened, and both of them heard the voice of the commander say, 'this is my beloved son in whom I'm well

pleased'. John was not sure until then….. until he saw him coming down the pathway towards the river for baptism. A great aura of beauty grew around him, and the peace of all heaven itself pervaded the very atmospheres; all were in the river waiting for baptism, and then John said, lord I cannot baptize you it is you who must baptize me. He said to me baptize me, for so it must be, but in so doing John, you send me out into all the world of man, not merely to our own people'

John had not been looking for a world messiah, but for a national Messiah. So overpowering was the beauty of that experience that John withdrew almost immediately, after having baptized Jesus. John went into the desert…… and then was my mission fulfilled. My disciples are blessed that they go with the lord Jesus, who had been anointed the Christ in the river Jordan, by John's hand. Why not rise with John….. we shall go further when next we are together, it is all for now. Thank you, Shalom, Shalom, Shalom.

John's uncertainty about the Messiah, and his own divinity, bear thinking about, because light channels are often very hard on themselves for not being constantly attuned to their divinity; yet here we have an advanced Avatar soul, who having left the paradise worlds of the supreme creator to undertake the earth experiment, experienced the same doubts about his divinity that we do.

During Jesus' many communications, he often gave 'snippets' about his time in Palestine that are not recorded in our Bible. Certain points that mankind has debated for years, were often casually clarified by him. The short excerpt below - concerning his origins and native tongue bears mentioning, for those who have enquiring minds. It seems that most artists/psychics who have 'seen' him, always depict him as having fair hair with blue eyes; this seems unlikely given the following information; ***Our origins were Asian, we were of the Sumarian and Assyrian races……. We spoke Aramaic, and many stories about us were recorded by scribes, often second hand. Most were recorded in Aramaic, for that was the language we spoke. Some manuscripts were written in Hebrew but eventually they were re-written in Latin, by the Greeks, therefore***

losing some of the deeper meanings. I was taught the Hebrew language, by the Essenes.

Throughout the tapes, many 'Gems of wisdom' are subtly dropped into general communications. Information has been given that Stonehenge is a magnetic vortex, linking earth with all the Zodiac houses. I have a deep intuitive sensing that the blue stones brought from Wales - comprising the inner ring of Stonehenge, may have something to do with the magnetic vortex. It has also been given that a great master lives in England at this time, and is re-activating the energy of the soul of Albion. Johnny volunteered the following information about CROP CIRCLES; ***They are made by the elemental kingdoms and the lords of Deveshan, under instructions from the creator Lords of light - the Elohim.*** On another occasion Ra ab Houtep said; ***A time is fast approaching when science will become religious, and religion will become scientific.***

The Mayans left behind signs for mankind to follow, one of which was a time calendar that began with the age of the sun in 1987. This calendar indicated energy shifts, and astronomical changes, that would be pointers for mankind to follow towards the end of the age of Pisces. The age of the sun, is a 25 year time cycle that man should take note of, concerning major earth changes, culminating in the year 2012. Interestingly, if one adds 25 years onto the time of the harmonic convergence in 1987, then the year 2012 pops up. Our tapes also confirmed that a major shift in consciousness occurred in 1987, as vast cosmic energies were directed to earth from the Zodiacal star houses, bringing earth into a higher vibration.

It will now become evident that we have undergone hundreds, or even thousands, of incarnations on earth, trying to reconnect to our pure godhood, and remember who we truly are.

(* Frequent references have been made about three Atlantian dispensations. Sometimes the Lemurian dispensation is referred to as the first Atlantian dispensation? It seems possible that the first Atlantian civilization was somewhere else on earth, at the same time as Lemuria, 51,000 years ago.)

(* This may refer to the second Atlantian dispensation which began 24,000 years ago in present day Egypt, and the Eastern Mediterranean.)

(* John constantly reminded the group that he was no different from them, and didn't like being referred to as 'My Lord'.)

(* Amy queried the terminology that John used when he said Jesus incarnated. John realized his error and clarified that he had used the wrong word - in that, his brother Jesus, never incarnated before that time. As an Avatar, Jesus created form bodies in many lands.)

Chapter 9

THE AVATAR

Bulawayo 1998

In August 2000, Kiran phoned me asking if I could visit an Australian couple who were night-stopping in Bulawayo. He was tied-up on stocktaking, and unable to meet them. I phoned them and arranged to pick them up in the afternoon. Brian was about 55 years of age, with short hair and a beard, and Lyn about 50. They were both fair haired with blue eyes, and very tanned from years spent on archaeological digs. The reason for their visit was to carry out an archaeological 'dig' in northern Zimbabwe. They were both Sai Baba devotees; they lived in Melbourne, and had got hold of Kirans name from the Sai Baba Africa headquarters, in Kenya.

They were both very open and friendly, as we hugged and introduced ourselves with the traditional Om Sai Ram greeting. I took them to the two houses that were manifesting vibhuuti, explaining how the manifestations had started, and the activities of the Sai group in Bulawayo, and the Orphanage in the Matopos. We returned to their private hotel, ordered tea, and the following story unfolded as to how they had come to know Swami;

Lyn; We are both archaeologists and often invited to different parts of the world, to carry out 'digs'. That's why we are here now. About five years ago, strange events occurred on our smallholding outside of Melbourne. At the time I wasn't working, but Brian was. I started hearing strange sounding chants and songs but whenever I moved towards the music to find the source, the sound would stop . . and then, later-on, I would hear it from somewhere else on the small-holding...... I could not pin it down, it just didn't make sense!

A close friend and neighbouring small-holder -Jean, often visited us. Jean was a lovely person, but a bit weird...... Brian and I often spoke about her 'new age' theories, which we could not relate to. We had been friends for many years, and she was my regular shopping partner, also Brian and her husband got on well. She came over for tea one morning, and before leaving dropped a book in my lap saying, 'you might find this interesting' I glanced at the book and smiled to myself; a fuzzy haired, dark skinned man, looked out from the cover of a book, that was entitled, My Baba and I. I put it on the table as we walked to our boundary fence, about a quarter of a mile away, arranging that we would go shopping on Friday.

The high pitched singing occurred nearly every day, it was so strange. One morning I knew the source to be our farm shed, about 150 yards from the house….. I walked towards it, the voice was definitely coming from the workshop, but when I got there, it suddenly started coming from the house? After about two weeks, I decided to broach the subject with Brian, who looked at me as if I was nuts. One evening we were sitting on the veranda, having a sun-downer, when he picked up Jeans book, glanced at the cover and started laughing. He looked at me and said, 'this must have come from Jean'.

I had forgotten about the book, and our conversation turned to Jeans egocentricities, we were very fond of her, so felt that we should at least glance through it - make an effort, so to speak. It was Saturday morning; Jean was visiting, and Brian was somewhere tending to our small herd of live-stock…… we light heartedly discussed our recent activities and local news. I was watering our vegetable patch at the time, as we planned our 'Barbie' for that evening. Shortly after Jean had left, Brian walked into the house looking confused he said, I heard it!.....but every time I walked towards the source, it mysteriously changed direction…. what the hell is it Lyn? I could offer no answers, but was glad that it was not my imagination. That evening as the men were burning the meat- bottles in hand, Jean asked if I had read the book she had left with me. I said, Jean I tried to, but it's just not believable…. It's not my cup of tea.

Two weeks passed, and we had still not solved the mystery of the music and singing on our small holding; it seemed to start and stop at different times, and then sometimes we wouldn't hear anything for a day of so. It was a Monday evening - I had gone into Melbourne for the day with Brian, and on arriving home, we discovered that Jean had left us a Video about Sai Baba. Our video player had been giving problems, so Brian took it in for repairs, arranging to collect it on Friday. Friday arrived but our video player was not ready, so we were given a loan set for the week end.

After supper we sat down to watch Jeans video which was entitled, God lives in India; half way through the video we looked at each other in disbelief. Sai Baba was leading a gathering, singing Hindu songs….. it was the same voice and music we had been hearing, for the past month! How could that be, we thought.

We paused the video and discussed it, then rewound it and played it all the way through, with a lot more attention to its content, and message. To say we were stunned was an understatement! We tried to rationalise the situation, but could not! We played the video two or three times again that week-end. I phoned Jean that evening, explaining to her what had been happening to us. She came over on Sunday with more books, and videos about Sai Baba; she smiled happily when we expressed our amazement at Baba's apparent communications with us.

Brian continued with the story……..Bob the amazing thing was that when I dropped the loan video player off the following Monday, the technician apologised profusely saying, 'My assistant put a customer's repair video on the 'loan shelf' in error…. we tried to phone you but your line was faulty, sorry if we wasted your time'. I assured him that the video had worked perfectly, and that there was no need to apologise; he looked at me sympathetically, then quickly took the cover off and pointed to the disconnected video head wires emphasising that it could not possibly have worked. For the second time in three days I was in total confusion. I mumbled oh I see. That's… strange?…. Umm……. When will our unit be ready?

From that time onwards, Jean and I knew we would be visiting Sai Baba in the very near future; in fact we were in India six weeks later. At our first Darshan, Swami stopped and said to Lyn, ***'So you are here, good'.*** When he reached the men's lines, he stood in front of me, and smiled. I could not believe the overwhelming energy of love that emanated from his eyes, it almost brought tears to my eyes. We have been devotees of Swami since that day, and visit him in Southern India, whenever we can. We have been privileged to have a number of personal interviews with him.

We promised to stay in touch with each other once they had finished their 'dig', but for some unknown reason, it did not happen and Kiran and I, never heard from them again. New information continued to come in about Swami, which the reader might find interesting, included below are a few transcripts;

Ra Ab Houtep - 3/11/94: ***Man's consciousness is rising to another level, where time as a factor, doesn't enter into it. Embyrionically, man is emerging as god - your scriptures tell you, YE ARE GODS.***

(Amy; Beloved one, if the Avatar is aware of the pattern of your life, is it because that person has rooted into him?)***No!..... the avatar is the Akashic - if Ra Ab Houtep can bring him down to that level he might not like it, he is the whole Akashic experience, incarnate.... that is why he knows everything about everybody. That is a very crude way of putting it, with apologies to your avatar.***

(Amy; He always says no one can understand me, you can only experience me.) ***Which is true, because your avatar – in that sense, is not an incarnate human being...... he is divinity incarnate - and potentially each one of you are, your scriptures say, 'Are ye not gods'; that is why he is able to call you, and his devotees. They respond to his teachings, and to his love, which is incarnate as him. He knows the exact level upon which each individual is operating.... and when a certain level within an individual is reached, he calls them consciously.***

(Dr; How do we make contact with the avatar)***You don't, he makes contact with you, and then there's no mistaking that contact, because you immediately feel a desire, to want to know more about him. You don't have to contact the Avatar, it's the other way around.***

(Dr; Like the father, contacts the son?) ***Because the father is us, the avatar is us -let us say, that is why he says it is not necessary for you to visit the physical aspect of him and his work in India, because he's there anyway. Wherever you are he's in your heart, that's where you make the contact, the kingdom of god within.***

Avon – 18/11/94; (during a thunderstorm) ***Greetings and blessings, it is Avon. Welcome to command Michael/Scorpio....***

Aries mid-station.... Mars/Earth (sound of thunder). ***It is good we have the thunder. This is a great power enclave at this moment...... it is Michael - command/ Scorpio, through the Antares command. At this particular time, it is the strong power energy of the Scorpio hierarchy, working under Michael, to bring to the Earth, a sense of restructuring of form, transmutation.***

At this time – the time of the incarnate avatar, these powers are mightily increased, for they earth themselves through the Avatar so to speak. The Avatar message at this time is to personalise the cosmic message, bringing into the affairs of the mental world of man's experience, the great transforming powers of transmutation. That is his message, transmute that within you that is less than perfect, to become perfect. (A loud thunder clap) ***Light channels must re-align the spiritual impulses that come 'thundering'*** (divine humour) ***from Cosmos. From the early days of man's history - in dealing with the spiritual hierarchies, great ones have come forwards again, and again, to gain more experience, in how to work with the zodiacal houses; they have undergone many incarnations, to learn their specific powers.***

You are being energized by the incarnate avatar in consciousness. Your period of preparation lies behind you, you have been blind flying and unaware of what was happening in your world, but that was because you needed to hone your own powers. Avon does not wish to say much at this time, except that you are working with the Avatar energies, of Pisces, and the fire energies of Scorpio, which are bringing about a tremendous power of rebirth, in your world. Great GREAT! is the power which grows in you, at this time. Your newly discovered ashram, in the great sub-continent, (Swami's ashram in India) ***extends at this time its tremendous love to you..... its recognition of you,.... its knowledge of you,..... its inclusiveness of you . We see the lights shining in the great mountains; we see the world encircled by great beacons of light..... the sound of gongs,.... the voice of worship, the chants of holiness. We see the great heart of love, and we join with it.***(Avon recited Dwaal Khuul's great invocation) ***Blessings and greeting, beloved ones, and beloved channel, lo we are with you always.***

Ra na ta - 22/9/93; ***God gave man two ears, and one mouth, in the hope that he would listen, twice as much as he talks.*** (divine humour) ***Michael's consciousness has incarnated, his feet walk your Earth.***

Ra Ab Houtep- 17/2/94; **Your avatar… Swami is unequalled love, and deep humanity.**

John - 22/9/94; ***There is a powerful new light impulse on earth, emanating from your incarnate Avatar. He is the incarnate Messiah, the ever coming one.***

Arel - 8/9/94; ***Prophecies have been made about a white horse . . Swami's car is white. He is of the Avatar soul group. . . He will not wave a magic wand for humanity. Sai Gita – the Avatars elephant, cries when he sees him, it sees and experiences only love. Incarnate man will become an Avatar, god is incarnate and omnipresent, as Swami.***

Ra Ab Houtep - 16/3/95; ***Because you know the truth of him, you are attuned to this cosmic avatar, and his ashram. He is the incarnate light; draw him into your hearts, and minds. Prepare for ascension, because the ever-coming one is Sai Baba.***

Johnny - 20/4/95; ***The dawn of the new age is here. It began with the incarnation of Swami; you don't have to touch him, or be in his presence, you meet with him in the silence. The reappearance of Christ is Swami, experience him!***

Jesus - 16/4/94; ***The darkness will be absorbed by the light…. you are confined in form but liberated in spirit. I lit my candle from the candle of all candles, the Cosmic Christ.***

Ra Ab Houtep - 27/4/95; ***Aquarius is the age of liberation. Man must go within to focus on his/her own divinity, then focus on your Swami. Vice and evil will cease to exist, you are close to that time now. Let the light forces deal with the dark forces….. live and call upon Swami, then they cannot touch you. Swami cannot be touched by negativity. Keep your faith, just bring him in.***

Dwaal Khuul - 16/11/95; ***Space command stations are alert. Welcome home brothers, and sisters, of light. We link in this moment, with the great ashram centre, in southern India.***

Johnny -1/2/96; ***There is staggering excitement ahead for all of us, and remember, Swami is in all situations. Love equals radiation...... hate equals disintegration. Become one mind with Swami, divinity has incarnated as love.***

Avon - 1/7/96; ***Sai is love incarnate - the cosmic incarnate mother,.... the divine feminine principal. He says do not look at my form, it is not me. To understand me, and find me, go within.***

Ra Ab Houtep - 11/7/96; George reads Psalm 46, then began channelling)***The lord god of hosts - mentioned in your holy book, is the incarnate Avatar. Sai is the god of Jacob. Dark powers are in retreat, world changes are very near..... and light channels are being swamped by Maya.*** (Illusion) ***Stop trying to assist others, stop it! Be detached. The divine Avatars energy force field, is very powerful, link to it, visualize him within you. God is incarnate in his creation; the Avatar is the great light, read Isaiah 9. I know you have difficulty with the way humanity treats animals.... man has choice..... let Swami handle it, in love. Put his face in all situations where animals are being mistreated. About two million years ago, you were under the commission of the golden ones from Regulus. Swami came to earth from Regulus, and now the golden ones are returning because of Swami, the cosmic Avatar of light, and love.***

Johnny - 28/11/96; ***Great events are unfolding for earth. Star fleets cannot come any closer, at this time - their energy and light is too powerful, these are the star-fleets of the Bai'nor. Energies are pouring into Swami, from these fleets; some channels can see them..... one day, all man will see the Regulus star-fleets, thanks to Swamis incarnation.***

Avon - 26/11/96; ***See the light corona from the photon belt; space fleet commands are very close to earth, and great beings are awaiting a spark from earth - from Swami. They cannot come nearer at this time, for they would shatter our lower bodies, until such time, as we raise our consciousness, and*** *vibration. The astral planes must be cleared of all negativity, before the star-fleets can come closer to earth. Molecular planetary changes will produce rattles, from the forces of darkness. The outer space planetary craft, contact earth through Swami. Do not interfere or advise others.... it short circuits the divine plan. Be detached; detachment doesn't mean lack of caring for a person, or situation, it means stand aside and see the illusion, for what it is. Allow to allow.*

Johnny - 29/5/97; ***Jesus, and Swami, are working from their cosmic god consciousness, on Earth. Talk to God - Swami, all the time. Light channels must put things into direct actions, by visualizations. Preshanti Nilyam, is the planetary heart centre. The increasing power of Prema love,*** (supreme love) ***is going out from Preshanti Nilyam, from Swami, the great divine incarnate. Prema love, is Prema Sai.***

Avon -30/10/97; ***Work as light, in the maya - but don't throw the baby out with the bath water. Atma, Christ, the Ruagh Hakudesh, equals your true source. Thought forms go out as spiritual energy. We are busy at this time with suicides..... you might call us the reception committee. Did you realize that Swami was a teenage Avatar, in the 2nd world war? Care for your fellow man in love, and remember you are god incarnate; live love from your source, like Swami.***

On the 13/7/95; Johnny came through with the following enlightening message, concerning the difference between the Avatar the Christ Jesus. ***I came down for a special purpose. I see confusion. No, that's not the right word; there's just a little bit of misunderstanding concerning this whole business of the Avatar and Jesus. If you like, we can do a bit of exploring around that point, with my own homespun, thrown in. It's good to remember that others have talked to you about the Christ office; we have talked to you about great beings, belonging to one special soul group who have from time to time, manifested themselves – descended into human bodies, to bring a special message at a special time.***

The Hindus have always had a concept of an Avatar, who is a total divine incarnation. The Hindu religion is much older

that anything known in the western world, and also many parts of the Eastern world. That doesn't mean to say that there haven't been great ones, coming down from the Christ office, to various other people, and incarnating and meeting them, on their level, at that time. Each of your major religions - during the past 2000 years or so, have had a concept of divinity, that came to mankind, at their particular time; this includes, the Budda, Lao Tsi, Confucious, and Zorester. Prior to that time, the lord Krishsna incarnated as an Avatar - a total divine incarnation - the purpose being to enlighten the planetary mind for that time and future times. Belonging to the Avatar group have been many well-known ones, from ancient Egypt, Babylon, and so on.

(Dr; When you say that an Avatar is a total divine incarnation, is there any difference between that and a manifestation from the office of the Christ?) ***Not a difference..... umm, a question of gradation. The Christ is in fact, the divine incarnation - as he came down, through Jesus, but you jumped the gun again. In the western world we use the word the Christ, generally speaking, in the Hindu world they use the term Atma, there is no difference. Isaiah could also be listed as coming from the Christ office; also many other saints, and prophets, in different parts of the world. All originated from the Christ office, but they graded their power down, for a specific purpose.***

(Dr; So Johnny, then the Avatar is a manifestation from pure spirit - as such, and the Christ is also a manifestation from pure spirit) ***Yes! But the office of the Atma - or the Christ, as it descended with the incarnation of Jesus, was a little different, in a sense that the Christ did not enter into him, at the birth of Jesus. The Christ descended, and overshadowed him, all the way through, prior to his birth; 'It' descended, at the baptism, in the river Jordan. You remember the story; they all went to be baptized, and a voice from everywhere said, this is my beloved son in whom I am well pleased. At that point the Christ actually took over. The physical vehicle of the lord Jesus, and the whole incarnate Christ office, became manifest in form, through him at that time. Jesus described himself as, the way-shower, the son***

of the father. With the incarnation of Jesus - and the overshadowing and indwelling of the Christ in Jesus, the avatar Christ spirit, entered into the very atomic structure of your planet, for the first time, as ordinary man.

(Amy; It's for the first time that he came as man, that is the big thing) ***YES! But still, the divine incarnation could no - at that time, incarnate in the body at birth, because the planet was not ready for it. All the other great religion - and the Hindus of course, have always had the ever coming one. The Buddah, the Jews, and later on, the Muslims, have all looked for a coming saviour. The Jews are still looking for their Messiah; the Imam Madi is yet to come.... the lord Matreya is yet to come, and so on. A cry has gone out, throughout the world, for the past two thousand years, saying, please father help. And now with this total divine incarnation, you have your Swami. When Jesus left he said, I will come again; he also said, I will leave with you the comforter. If you want to interpret the word com-fort, it means, come forth, the one who would come forth. Unless I go the comforter, I will not come to you, but I will return, he said. He is the only one of the Avatar group that has returned as the Avatar, or as the Christ, if you wish. The soul has cried out throughout the world for him to return and he is returning.***

The purpose of this divine incarnation - the Avatar your Swami, will unite the entire world in a bond of love. You don't need to belong to something, or become anything different, from what you chose to be; he himself has said, the Buddhists had to grow as a group, and the Jews as Jews, and the Christians as Christians, the Hindus as Hindus, the Taoists as Taoists, and so on. So there is no difference at all, because the message of each one of them - in its essence, is exactly the same, love one another, as I have loved you.

(Amy; Johnny, you've talked about the father, could you explain that because you didn't say he was the father, but Swami says he is the father) ***It is claimed for him particularly, that he is the total divine incarnation - the father aspect, the initiator, the protector, whereas Jesus claimed to be the son. He was also god as such, but as your Swami says, so are you. He says, the only difference***

between you and me is that I know it, and it's about time you woke up, and know it. It is a great divine being-ness that has incarnated, using a human vehicle, in order to contact man, planetary wise.

Jesus couldn't do it planetary-wise because the world was a much smaller place in his day. Now, Jesus returns to be the fulfilment of the law and the prophets; the message that he gave then, is what your Swami is giving today, there is no difference. What your Swami has done, is to re-activate the spiritual soul of the mother of all religions, to rekindle, and revitalize what was given by Krishna, and the other avatars...... He says he is their incarnations - and as an Indian avatar, he is. The points of view or difference between Jesus, and Swami, are manmade. It doesn't matter what you call love, love is love; you can dress it up in any name you like, but it's still love. Your Swami has incarnated as divine love, and wisdom; he doesn't say get close to me, he says get close to god within you, however you see your god. He says, whatever your traditional background is regarding god, go to him, deep inside, because there you'll find me also. Is it clearer now, or not much clearer?

(Dr; Johnny I don't visualize a being, I feel the father) ***Yes that's what it is. Are you clear now about the Avatar, and Jesus? God has come, because man has called out for god, and each one of them has come to represent god in their own way, to represent god as; the father, Jesus, the Imam Madi, the Messiah, Guru Dev, the lot. The great Guru, the only Guru, is God. I came down to talk to you, because I felt that there was non-clarity in your minds. I was just visiting so thought I'd pop-in; I'm making contact with people who are making the great trek,*** (people who have passed on) ***I've needed to help them.***

(Amy; Thank you for dropping in) ***Well I'll do it again, and the next time I come through and you want to talk about something on this level, we can talk. We bless your footsteps and the days that lie before you, and your families, and your children, and children's children, and everybody. Blessing and greetings beloved ones, beloved sisters and brother.***

In the above communication, Johnny spoke of gradations of consciousness in relation to Jesus, and Sai Baba. Jesus and John said in their communications, that they came from their father's house, to Earth, and then they suggested that their father was one of the Elohim! The father that sent them is the Cosmic Christ of our universe and is influencing the whole of Earth, is BHAGAWAN SRI SATHYA SAI BABA. Our Bible says in prophecy that the Christ will return from the East, and indeed, the cosmic Christ lived in Southern India, as the Avatar of love.

The human mind tries to slot God, Jesus, Avatars, Archangels etc, into cubby-holes, not realizing that in essence, all is one. God is one. We are ONE as beings of light, and always will be, despite our brief embodiments into physical forms. Sananda, Sai Baba, Michael, Melchizadek, and many other beings involved with the Earth experiment, are of the Avatar soul group. The ultimate sacrifice that an Avatar can make is to incarnate; they can transmute their divine consciousness into physical form, and walk amongst us. They do not have to suffer the indignities of being looked after, as a helpless baby: They do it only, TO SHOW US THAT WE TOO ARE GOD. Jesus said 'Things that I do, you can do, and even greater things.

Chapter 10

GOD

CHRISTIANITY and the Bible. SPIRITUALITY and the ancient wisdom teachings.

I made reference earlier in this book to the first and second Nicene council meetings that took place in Rome around 330 AD. This event was during the reign of Constantine - in fact he initiated it, because the holy Roman church expressed concern to him that their texts were different in certain key areas from other Christian churches throughout Europe and the misty isles. All churches possessed their own manuscripts and sacred texts that had been transcribed from other texts or written as events witnessed by people first hand. Some manuscripts were records of retold stories by other people, and faithfully recorded. In essence, many of these texts told similar stories or gave similar explanations of spiritual or religious events that had occurred on earth during the previous 11500 years.

Many of the old-testament manuscripts were originally written in Aramaic, Hebrew or Coptic. Later on many were re-transcribed into Latin and English. The Essenes sent their original texts to Europe and the misty isles shortly after Christ's resurrection and then re-wrote them as the dead-sea scrolls. Much truth was lost between the original manuscripts and the dead-sea scroll texts. It is a question in some instances, of reading between the lines or trying to understand the deeper meanings behind the messages. It has been given on our tapes that the Bible has seven different levels of understanding or meanings.

Returning to the first Nicene meeting, there was major disagreement on The Trinity - God the Father, God the Son, and God the Holy Ghost. After many weeks of non-agreement between the different Christian churches, Constantine stepped in and a common understanding was reluctantly agreed to because the Roman church and ruling Roman Empire apparently possessed more manuscripts than the other churches. It should be remembered that he Romans were the empire builders who controlled most of the middle-East, Europe and the misty isles at that time so it was only logical that the other churches conceded to their understanding because of the military power and wealth of available evidence that the Roman church had.

There were many ancient wisdom teachers in Palestine before and at the time of Jesus; they were drawn to that land by divine inspiration, (inner circle knowingness) some, like the three wise men, came from the East. Other enlightened beings came from Europe, Egypt, Greece, the east and the misty isles. They took their manuscripts back to their lands as new revelations about the Christ for their race groups. The Druids, Celts, Greeks and the sacred temples of learning in the Himalayas would all have their own version of events leading up to and including the unfolding drama of Jeshua Ben Joseph. Highly trained initiates, who understood the deeper truths of god/goddess, divinity, the soul, etc, would write about those events in their native tongues which were faithfully kept by their people. Certain words such as reincarnation, Prana and Karma were fully understood and accepted from the written records in the various languages at that time.

The Roman church hierarchy and elders of the Roman Senate studied these 'other' Bible texts at a 2nd Nicene council meeting; once again many manuscripts in different languages were laid on the table and became the subject of heated debate as to who possessed the ultimate truth. Sadly, the 2nd Nicene council meeting also agreed to remove certain words and texts from the original manuscripts; partly because they did not understand what they really meant. Adding to this, Pope Pius the first also re-wrote some of the original texts and removed parts which showed all men as being equal and one with god.

In earlier texts, reincarnation was frequently mentioned as man's embodiments on earth as a soul being. References to the feminine aspect of god were also removed because when Jesus spoke of 'his father' they felt that God must be male. Certain manuscripts that clearly indicated man and women's divinity were intentionally removed. Modern theologians disagree on scripture daily; one example is the fact that the bible clearly states 'I of myself can do nothing, it is the father within that doeth the works'. I of myself, clearly relates to the human form and mind of man/woman, and 'the father within' is our, I AM presence or soul. Debates on subjects such as 'In my father's house are many mansions' end up in total disagreement as to its real meaning; other hot topics such as, God is in the congregation, or know ye not ye are gods were seldom agreed on. By removing words like Karma and reincarnation, the various churches have been able to exercise more control over their congregations, for if mankind only had one lifetime on earth, then they had better get it right by tithing, obeying, and supporting their churches or else!

The word Prana - derived from ancient Sanskrit - was the nearest explanation to understanding what the holy breath was. (Ancient Hebrew documents referred to it as the Ruagh Hakudesh.) It is now known that Constantine's Roman church and advisors had many other gospels to choose from such as; the gospel of Mary of Magdala, Joseph of Aramethea, Miriam, Thomas, Philip of Greece, Nicodemus, Mother Mary, Andrew, etc. Constantine and the holy Roman church advisers selected the gospels that we know today because they seemed to have similar explanations about the life and times of the master, Jesus.

The following information was given by Johnny on the 24/1/02; ***The Christian world has governed the so called civilization of the planet for over 1700 years and all the other religions have had to fall into line.... because they used the power of money to keep control,..... economics if you like. This brought about a violent, rigid and merciless control of human beings...... This is a bit rough isn't it?***

(Amy; It gives us what the issues are beloved one.) ***You can read all about it in the first and last chapters of your book*** (The Bible) ***which has been edited many times and all too often misinterpreted many times as well. The only differences between man and man, and man and god, are man-made! The pendulum has swung bringing the harbingers of truth into the feminine court.... most of your teachers of truth in these times, are women not men; this is swinging the pendulum in the age of Aquarius, towards the balancing of the masculine and feminine***

principle. There are also men of course, but by and large the ladies are setting the pace into this new Aquarian age. I'm not telling you or giving you anything new today.... I'm just putting into some sort of context, the suppression of truth during the past age of Pisces. It has been religious suppression, not a spiritual one.

The ancient Egyptians kept their own sacred records and teachings going back to 10,000 BC. These writings would be brought to the promised land by the priesthood of Levi, the Gnostics and the Essenes, who would continue to record events up until their total disappearance from the desert 60 years after Christ's crucifixion. Many left within a few years of this event because of the persecution by Herod, the Sanhedrin priesthood, and the occupying Roman forces. Some of these teachings would find their way to a powerful new centre of light at Glastonbury, about 9,500 years ago. Many of the Celts and Druid communities in England and Ireland, received new impulses of light, at the time that the Essenes left Palestine, about 1,950 years ago. I believe that one such group would become known as the Esceni; an army led by Queen Boadicea, challenged the Roman occupation of England at that time, but were defeated. Is it not interesting that no one has put two and two together concerning the similarity of the word Essene, and the Esceni of England?

The Nag Hamadi texts discovered in a small village outside of Cairo, contained many ancient Essene, Gnostic, and old-testament teachings, linked to an early Hebrew communities that lived throughout Egypt, and on the Island of elephantine, 2500 years before the birth of Jesus. The information contained within these texts conflict with beliefs held in the Torah and the Bible and are therefore rejected out of hand, by the Jews and Christians alike - better the devil you know!

From the perspective of what I have said so far, Isaiah 45 Verse 7 makes very interesting reading, because of the many modern interpretations of what 'God' apparently said, in the different Bibles available today - about 115 versions! Here are a few of the various interpretations of what Isaiah apparently said?

(a) I create the light, and I create the darkness, I create good, and I create evil, I the lord thy god create all of these things.

(b) I form the light and create darkness, I bring prosperity and create disaster, I the lord, do all of these things.

(c) I form light and make darkness, I make weal and woe, I make peace and create darkness,

(d) I make peace and create evil I create both light and darkness, I bring both blessings and disaster.

(e) I make light, I create darkness, author alike of prosperity and trouble.

On the 18/8/93, the master teacher Ra-ab Houtep came through giving deeper insights into God, and good and evil. Once again I have only taken pertinent extracts of his communication; ***Ra-ab Houtep would like to simply talk to you this time. Yes thank you. Ahh we have visitors moving in as well.*** (Discarnate souls drawn to the sanctuary) ***We welcome you. I want to talk about the great power that resides within each one of you. You have all been told, and have acknowledged, that there is really only one god; that god is one, but is all. Many queries have come into your minds, for if god is one, then what is god, if god is all powerful, why do we see evil around us? If god is all powerful, surely there can't be evil as well. Evil is that which man has created, and cannot exist in reality. Evil therefore, does not exist; it is a state of affairs that has been accepted by mankind, as being normal and inevitable, and in the acceptance thereof, lies the power for that illusion, to manifest itself. This is not what god conceived of because man was given the free will faculty, and is able to choose.***

You can walk through your world in the midst of evil, without it touching you in any way whatsoever, because you will not allow it to draw you away from what you know your god is. Illusion, and violence, applies to the earth scene, and the times in which man is living. You see evil around you, but it should not affect you, unless you engage the ears of emotion. Evil was there in the beginning and has to be fed otherwise it would pass out of man's experience. But, this is not the case with good. God/good does not have to assert itself, it is simply there; it has about itself, a recognisable permanence which you call truth; it

does not need any form of identification at all - it simply is, because it is god. The good-God that was there in the beginning continues to be there for those who seek it but, evil has to be constantly re-created because it is what man has made of the power.

You are living in an illusion..... your very human strivings will pass away,..... but the word - which is god, will not pass away. God is the presence within you, you cannot find god outside of yourself, only within; in any situation that you find yourself in, simply say Father thy will be done. Your young friend of many years ago (Johnny) ***would often say to you, 'you have your own built-in do it yourself kit'. In creation god/good, and evil, exist side by side, but it is still god.***

As incarnate gods, we have indeed perpetuated good and evil actions on earth. Sadly those that have seen themselves as wiser or more learned than us, have totally overlooked this fact! GOD did not say I AM EVIL, he apparently said? I CREATE EVIL - or more correctly, within my creation the sons and daughters of god, create good and evil. Over the years our more enlightened Christians teachers, mistook that verse as meaning, god is evil; this has happened so many times during the past 1700 years, during which the ancient Bible truths have become adulterated.

Research into the LORDS PRAYER also makes interesting reading, in that the original Aramaic texts bear little or no resemblance to our modern Bible interpretations. It seems to me that as a means of making women less than men, god became 'Our Father who art in heaven'. The actual translation from the original Aramaic text is; Oh Birther of the cosmos, may your name be held in awe.

Our tapes tell us that man/woman was with god in the beginning and that we were created in the image and likeness of god, male female alike. It is unlikely that the master Jesus saw women as less than man, when he spoke to the congregations; 'the song of Mirium'- a very high initiate, and one the first to visit the tomb after his crucifixion shows clearly that Mirium spoke on behalf of the Master, when he addressed the congregation at the well! Surprisingly, that event seems to have been left unchanged from the original manuscripts. Our one-ness with god - as spiritual beings, encompasses the first principle of Love/Wisdom, which is God/Godess, and all that is.

Avon gave this discourse in a communication dated August 2001; ***This is a great opportunity to work with the energies of the solar logos in Leo, and the cosmic virgin mother energies, in Virgo, uniting the divine masculine, and the divine feminine, on earth. The Cosmic Mother is the feminine balance in Virgo. It is the divine mother who produces the bodies in creation; this has been the great message, in all your religions. The divine feminine principle, has been worshipped under many names, the greatest, and fulfilling of them all, being Mary of Bethlehem. It is because of these powerful energies, that your Christian church was formed. It does not matter what has transpired due to man's free will or what man has done with these energies throughout the centuries….. only that the divine masculine, and the divine feminine were incarnate at the same time, through your lord Christ Jesus, and Mary of Bethlehem, who represented the Cosmic mother, in Virgo.***

I would like to make it very clear to the reader, that divine minds understanding of our Bible, does not in any way attempt to discount the overall wisdom, and truth, within some of its many chapters and verses. Many entities that have come through, gave detailed inner teachings on certain old-testament texts such as, Job, Psalms, Enoch, Isaiah, Genesis etc. I do not therefore make a blanket claim that all content within the Bible is incorrect. The debate on translation of many Bible texts continues to this day, with very little -if any, agreement.

I was listening to Southern Counties radio the other day, where the presenter interviewed two Bishops who attended the Lambeth conference of Christian bishops. The presenter delicately referred to the problem of gay bishops, which seemed to be breaking up the Christian church. A theologian said, the scriptures that the American and African bishops interpret, are the same that we use in England and Europe…. 'We must somehow come to terms with the interpretation of scripture'. Another said, 'The difference in trying to understand and interpret scripture has caused much pain in the Christian community'. An understatement!

SPACE CITIES/BIOSPHERES OF LIGHT – Mother-craft and UFO'S

In addition to the information already given, I include in this section part extracts on this controversial - yet interesting, subject channelled by many entities over the years. For thousands of years mankind has seen things in the skies; some have recorded them on cave walls, or legends of them, have been passed down through different root races, to present times. During the past 60 years, more and more of humanity, have seen flying objects in our skies, which apparently, appear and disappear, at will. They have variously been described as huge cigar shaped objects, mother-ships, UFO's, flying saucers etc. I have given insights for the sudden appearances or disappearances of these craft, in earlier chapters, in relation to transmutation.

Within the environs of our solar system, and more recently closer to earth, are numerous space cities - biospheres of light that recently arrived from beyond the mazzaroth houses, via the gateways of Arcturus, Orion, Alpha Centauri etc, in preparation for mankind's leap into cosmic consciousness, which is ascension. These craft are of the Bai'nor light fleets, and are inter universal space cities and scientific laboratories. They are mind controlled etheric craft, therefore invisible to human eyes; they can however transmute into physical craft. Our Zodiacal houses each have one of these vast mother-ships, which moved into our star houses at the onset of the earth experiment, millions of years ago. The powers of darkness have their own craft which have been used to oppose the light, and the experiment of earth. They have produced robot/clone entities, responsible for physical mutilations, and abductions of humanity.

Nearer to earth, and above the Siankang desert extending into Mongolia, is the etheric city of SHAMBALLA - home of the brotherhood of light. Shamballa is also called the NEW JERUSALEM and 'the centre that we call the race of men - as given by Dwaal Khuul, in the Great invocation. Some Mother-craft within the environs of our solar system have only recently been able to draw nearer to Earth since it went into a higher vibration at the time of the harmonic convergence in 1987. These etheric craft have scout-ships -

commonly referred to as flying saucers which are able to move within our solar system and the Galaxy.

On the 30/8/84 Archangel Gabriel spoke of these craft saying that a time would come when the raised consciousness of mankind would make it possible for them to come even nearer to earth. Gabriel took the group on a visualization journey to Gamma Virginus in the Constellation of Virgo: ***Let us move down this passageway to the great windows that lie before you; look out across the galaxy, and you will see the scintillating orange rays of mighty Arcturus. These rays are reflections, which come to us from beyond the gates, heralding the arrival of the sons of light, the great Bai'nor. When they enter into this part of the Galaxy, they wing their way through the stars, towards your solar system. It is from Gamma Virginus - in this complex, that they will make their move.***

As man begins to purify himself, and regains his virginal state of consciousness, he meets with the Bai'nor. Those who are the vanguard of mankind, shall conduct them towards earth, the great mother craft of the Bai'nor fleet, lies yet beyond the gateway of Arcturus, (this changed around 1996) ***because it is too vast to enter. Many of the scouting vessels have already entered, as you know. These craft are large as viewed by your earth.***

The negative powers operating out of Alpha Draconus, and Saturn, became less intrusive to earth from 1995/96; Earth was largely sealed off from their experiments with human beings, and animals. A Ring pass not was placed around earth, when Archangel Michael opened the Astral planes with his symbolic sword of light; 'He sealed the door where evil dwells', as given by Dwall Khuul in his Great Invocation. The dark lodge, were forced to return to their constellation of Alpha Draconus and Saturn, OR incarnate on Earth. Despite the fact that some of the negative forces operate out of Saturn, it is considered to be the planet of transformation for earth; it is also where the lords of karma are based.

The Libbie's, E/Ts, or Grey's, hope to perpetuate their own race on earth, after our solar system's re-entry into the Photon belt. These entities have no emotional bodies and part of their experiments with humanity, were carried out to try and create one. They are robot-like and controlled by the dark powers who were not prepared to go through the sacrifice of en-soulment of earth like we did. Strangely, it seems that some ET's are benign to humanity but, since 1997, their interference with Earth's life forms have been curtailed; the Christ office took free will and choice away from them for the first time since the experiment of Earth began. The negative forces can still manifest their scout-ships within our solar system but even that will slowly diminish, for they must first pass the legions of light.

The following description of the etheric mother craft - referred to as Shamballa, was given to the group by Arel; ***It is about 250 miles long, 30 miles wide, and 10 miles high; it can sustain physical human life, on a higher vibration....***(etheric/physical life) ***It is a space city world with mountains, rivers, lakes and fields of agriculture. It supports etheric seed forms that live a life similar to your earth forms, but they are etheric/physical. It has a large City and smaller villages.... and clouds which bring rain and light that flood the whole land to nurture the life forms. It is not the same light as your Sun, this light comes from the etheric life forms of this world. Shamballa cannot be seen by human eyes; planes flying through it have no awareness of it, apart from slight magnetic disturbances to the planes instruments. Shamballa is tiny compared to the vast bio space cities of the Bai'nor which are anchored in your Zodiac houses.***

I will now offer the reader an amazing insight into an event that occurred during a BBC radio phone-in program, about 27 years ago. I first became aware of 'the incident' when Harold Broomberg leant me a tape which gave details of the event in which, a senior BBC official at that time gave his views on what had occurred. Apparently, during the phone-in program on the probability of extra-terrestrial life, an entity calling itself 'Asteron' by-passed the BBC switchboard control system and communicated direct with the presenter on air! I believe this created quite a buzz amongst the British public at the time? The following tape begins with Johnny introducing a being called Althor, who gave the following communication.

Johnny 19/5/83; ***We're going to go for a ride in an explorer craft, not the big one.... a scout ship. This consciousness will take us on-board - we'll be the guest of the captain. Greetings,*** *you are welcomed aboard the craft.... it is Althor. I give you the name Althor because it is the nearest I can come into your earth pronunciation.*

Thank you, welcome,.... would you close those hatches, thank you. Welcome aboard, you small select crowd. I see some of you have met..... Oh! I see you haven't? I see..... umm. You have met on your inner planes of consciousness, but not physically. That to us is not incomprehensible, but we smile a little to think that people as close as you on this vibration, could not have come into contact, in your earth life experiences.

Mine was the scout ship that you have been viewing lately over this part of your planet (South Africa). *We would like you to ask your questions. Oh.... I see? Some of you are in physical form and others of you are not. Let us rise.... as we move backwards from your plane, see the moon, mercury, and your other planets. Now look at your solar system; we are half way between Alpha Centauri and your system..... look at the stars and the play of the universe before you.*

Yes, thank you..... yes we are. The question from that brother of yours was, are we one of many craft? Yes we are (a telepathic communication was taking place between Althor, and someone else on the craft?) *Yes...... We are anchored within the mother craft at this time; you might liken it to a miniature planet. I'd like to say at the outset that our mission to your planet is one of love and deep fellowship, and to communicate with you at soul consciousness. We are of the brotherhood of light and the Christ office; therefore you are safe with us for we acknowledge the same source and origin. There are other powers less disposed to man who would seek to enslave you for they do not wish you to evolve spiritually. They work in similar craft in your solar system from the planet of Saturn; they are your sisters and brothers but have chosen materialism.*

(Amy; Are these the ones that are harming the human race, by taking people away against their will?) *Yes these are the ones, but remember light dispels the darkness, so they cannot win the hearts and minds of man, for he has woken up to his divine origins, as a being of love and light.*

(Amy; We have heard a rumour that some Japanese people have been taken to a twin planet called Epicot - to work there. Is that a true story?) ***Let us say this is a very involved topic. There are individuals who have come from our own star-ship, and have entered into the world, of man-kind. It is difficult for us to convey to you in your terms, the exactness of ourselves and our position. Epicot is the name of one of our craft that has been working with the technology of the peoples that you call Japan. They have taken-on for themselves human forms among these people, and also the characteristics of these people; that is why the relayed broadcasts which you have had back have intonations which seem to be peculiar to either one section of people, or another - in this case, your Japanese.***

Just as the powers of darkness are working with technology, so are we. You may have the assurance that this contact, is of the light. Our junior craft meet in the city craft, with peoples of earth, who talk in different languages. On our plane of existence, we do not have a diversity of language, we communicate telepathically. It is extremely difficult for us to convey to you, how we transfer, teleport, and experience, one dimension to another; and even more difficult when we have to contact you, with words - on your material physical plane, because its limitations, are excruciating. Our task is to raise your level of communication, to that of our mental telepathic level.

(Amy; The man Asteron, who was talking on the British broadcasting corporation, was that a genuine contact?) ***Yes, there have been a number of cases, where there have been interrupted broadcasts; that is done deliberately by some of us to get people to think and make them aware of the presence..... of ourselves, and thus prepare them to come forwards, to meet us. You would be quite surprised at the number of enlightened individuals on your planet - in high places, who are in direct contact with us, but await the right timing. Your gentleman over there.... Britain you said..... There is a man on our craft who is very high up, in the...*** (I cannot divulge further information for ethical reasons.)

Oh! He says he knows what is going on, and it is not the first time he has visited my craft..... Oh, you have been in four other craft. You see there are a number in your world..... oh, physically. He wants me to tell you that he is here now physically - that he is still in physical form. Oh!.... you've been in five craft, and now in my craft.

Unlike our other brothers, we do not force people to enter our craft, we invite them in if they wish, and give them full protection to enter. There have been a number of occasions, when we have contacted people of your earth, where the communication level is strong between us; we have invited some to come and stay with us, for one, or other reason, usually because of their commitment under karma, to earth people, they feel that they must remain with Earth. These people are usually individuals from our solar system, who have incarnated in man's world, to undergo certain experiences. They do not belong to your planet.... intuitively they know they do not belong here.

(Amy; Beloved one, those who go physically into your craft, are they on another vibration?) ***What would you say my friend?*** (Althor talking to the 'guest' from England) ***Ah yes.... He said -like the poet, it is like a sleep and a forgetting. What he means is, that in his consciousness, he came into the craft and then his body undergoes a process of transmutation - as does everything which is physical within the craft, so that we can travel inter dimensionally. When he returns he has a slight period where he sleeps and forgets - so to speak, where his body re-adjusts itself, then once again he is in his physical vehicle..... Althor would like to stress at this point that your purpose in life - in the human world, is to develop your spiritual qualities, not your psychic gifts.***

When you have arrived at a point where you are able to communicate inter dimensionally, you will have developed a very strong spiritual nature; the love and intelligence factor, must unite as consciousness within you, with no sense of duality, or separation. You must know – as your words say, that I and the father are one, and to serve in pure love, and light. Before this can be done, your astral planes - beginning with

your own vehicle, must be purified. Yours is a spiritual mission, to develop the consciousness of the great father within you. However exciting our little jaunts might be, they are but jaunts, until you learn to communicate with your real self. In the meantime, we shall continue to communicate with you, until you are aware of the great power.

Look out at the Universe; we are travelling around your solar system, look at the beautiful colours..... See that glow near earth, that is moving towards your moon, that is our mother craft. This celebration is a most powerful one indeed, your Christ energies are being focused on at this time. Let us enter into the landing stage of our mother craft; we enter a lighted tunnel, and slow down..... the doors open, and we enter into the foyer of the great craft. There is your ray descending to the earth, just step into that ray .... that's right. Au' revoir.

(Johnny) ***Thank you, Althor.... Captain Althor. Gee that was quiet a journey. Let's take our consciousness down now shall we, down to earth?...... That's quite a craft.... with those twelve entry.... airports, you might call them.***

Let us look at the implications of this visualization visit, in Althor's craft. Firstly the Arel group, were raised to a higher consciousness and vibration by Johnny, who told them that they were going on a space journey. Then he handed over to Althor - in the scout craft, which was a conventional flying saucer. Johnny's consciousness left the channel, and Althor took over - with permission from the channel, at soul level. The group 'were brought' into Althor's craft, at a level of, soul, mental, etheric consciousness, not physically. Interestingly, there was one other person on the craft physically - an Englishman, who was assisted to transmute his physical body into a higher etheric vibration adaptable for space travel.

The Englishman was probably picked up by agreement somewhere in England, and entered the craft physically; he was then assisted to transmute his physical body, into a higher vibration. A three-way communication ensued between the group, the Englishman, and Althor. The group would not have heard the Englishman's communications or explanations, but Althor did, at telepathic level, which he then passed on to the group. Whilst all this was going on, the craft had moved 100 light years from earth, towards Alpha Centauri! Althor's communication was primarily for the Arel group - a divine question and answer session, but whoever else was on the craft, would have heard Althor's telepathic communication with the group, but not Amy's human voice questions. So as with the communication from the Englishman, Althor would have explained to him- telepathically, Amy's communication.

It is sad that our separation from divine mind has made us forget our inter-dimensional consciousness and telepathic communicating ability, for at a spiritual mind level, we know it all. The time has come for us to raise our consciousness and awareness to our divine truth - in that, for thousands of years we have experimented at **being human,** and are finally realizing that we are indeed divine adventurers, and that earth is not our real home.

The following communication came through from Ra-na-ta, on the 22/9/93. I have only transcribed part of his communication. ***Greetings blessings it is Ra-na-ta. Without formality shall we ascend. Let us find ourselves in our observation room,*** (in the Etheric City of Shamballa) ***with its familiar room, and windows. You are left suspended in space somewhere beyond your moon. See before you -on your screen, your earth, your moon; now let us move back, as you spiral your way out of your solar system. Let us move out into the galaxy of your milky way and then back further, until you see a spiral of stars. Let's move further back, until your milky way recedes to become almost like a star, a large star, yes? Now look beyond, and behind, and you will see many such stars; they are part of this universe, they are Galaxies, can you comprehend this? One of those stars that you can hold in your hand, is a galaxy so vast as to be un-measurable by you. There are countless millions of solar systems involved in each of these stars..... and countless more millions of planets. This exists, even your telescopes of earth have picked up this information, ah..... and space lies in between.***

(Amy; In the etheric?) ***On its various levels. Conceive now that you are in the centre of your Universe; around you lie countless*** *thousands of stars, which are galaxies, yes? Let your imagination play upon this..... this is but one universe of created physical matter, parts of which your earth telescopes have seen and recorded on photographs. Let us move out of the centre of this universe shall we? As we move.... look at your screen..... you can see that all of these stars seem to be coming closer together - decreasing in size. As we move back further out - or perhaps further in, see how those thousands of stars are becoming one star, the size of a ball, that you can hold in two hands. Now look beyond and around you, and you will see other stars of similar size; there are more than you can count at a glance, these are Universes, containing countless thousands, and millions, of galaxies, solar systems, and planets.*

You are looking at part of your created universes, in manifest form. You must forgive Ra-na-ta if he labours this point; try to grasp the magnitude of what comprises the worlds in which you move, and live, and have your being. Now let us remember, there never has been a time, when man was not. You must say, before all the worlds of creation, I AM. Ra-na-ta will take things slowly with you, but you must ask your questions. Remember - independent of form, time, and space, I AM. You are more eternal than all the universes that Ra-na-ta has shown to you on the screen, you are eternal, and all this is not! Can you conceive of this? You are spiritual beings, in all the majesty of your own right, and all of this, was created by god.

Avon gave the following information on the 6/12/85; once again I have only taken excerpts from his message; *Greetings, come in Avon's craft to Sagittarius, where we will visit Gamma Epsilon. See the great corona in the sky. By-passing Sigma, and Epsilon, we dip below the Corona Australia's, towards the great spiral of your milky way - the inner galactic ring* (The vortex at the centre of our galaxy). *We follow this ring towards the northern galactic pole, and then to one of the arms of your galaxy, an arm of stars going off from it. We will keep your solar system on our mind controlled computer screen, so that you can compare it with the solar system we are visiting now...... Is it not vast and beautiful?*

As we swing around the spiral, look down into the vortex; you will see pure radiant light, which is the womb of your galaxy, and out of sight to you. Near the galactic South Pole, is your tiny little solar system. We move out on this arm of your galaxy, towards a binary star system, with its planets; your astronomers cannot see this system with their telescopes, there is too much cosmic dust and gas fields, in-between. Your solar systems sun is variable, and might soon send out pulsations - flames, that will go beyond earth and Jupiter….. and might destroy earth, making it a dead planet.

This binary star system, (Two suns) *polarize each-others energy. One sun is of a blue/green radiance, and the other an orange/red radiance, like your sun. These suns polarize each-others energy, they are stable and in perfect balance with each other. This is home; your next experience in galactic consciousness and life is in that beautiful binary system. There is a planet in this system that is ready to receive man; in truth you have lived on this planet before, either in physical or etheric form. Between incarnations you have come home to this solar system many times - as etheric soul man, you will return to - let's say, number seven planet when the earth experiment is over.*

In the beginning, the experiment of earth was under the control of the brotherhood of light, who en-souled several of your planets, as a challenge to see if they could raise their consciousness, within a violent solar system, in a physical body. Because of your suns instability, the experiment of earth was interfered with by galactic scientist. This would not have been possible, if your solar system had balancing binary star; therefore the polarizing energies of you system, were centred in one unstable sun, which caused earth movement, and destructive periods. The negative powers used these destructive periods, to bring forth their powers in matter, and consolidated them on your planets - Saturn mainly, and especially your earth. Despite this, you accepted to come to grips with violent matter, and learn from it.

As divine mind incarnate, you learned to evolve within your system, this is why you have the knowledge of good, and evil. Avon felt that he had to explain to you, why there is so much suffering, on your planet. Saturn has had to bring about balance, within the imbalance, of your system. The great lords of Saturn, instituted the law of balance, within your solar system, for as it sowed negative energy, it also reaped negative energy, to the extent that its scientists failed to control the light by fear, domination, and interference, with the earth experiment.

Your cosmos is open now to receive the sun of Kolob and you will pass through a null zone,(the Photon belt) *during which all life on your planet will undergo a complete and entire change which will be Ascension into a higher vibration - a new heaven and earth. At the moment, you are in a time warp approaching the peak of another wave, then you will become freed and liberated, forever. ARE YOU NOT GODS?!..... You are the higher lords, my beloved ones. Our sun* (Earth's sun) *has an 11 to 17 year pulsation cycle which shrivelled the planets nearest to it - and also our moon - millions of years ago; depriving them of their life forms. This will happen again but assistance from galactic scientists can nullify the effects to a certain extent, more importantly, man's raised consciousness will also nullify the effects.*

The Photon vortex from Kolob, will absorb its photon energy back to itself - switch it off so to speak. (At this point, there was inter-communication with Thias - Avon's 'sister', on Gamma Epsilon.) *Yes ... Thias has reminded me, that the white horses were brought to earth from Gamma Epsilon, and man abused them in warfare, as killing machines. See our white cows?.... We took them to India; the population saw us bringing them down to earth in our craft, and ever since, the Indian race memory has remembered that they were a gift from god. They saw us come down from the heavens, and release the cows in their land. There is no violence on our planet,*(Gamma Epsilon)*because our two suns polarize each other sending out harmonious energy; unlike your sun which pulsates destruction to its planets. Had Sanat Kumar not en-souled your sun billions of years ago, it*

would have destroyed itself and the planets. If he had not controlled his sun, the earth experiment would have ended a long time ago. My sister Thias has asked her mate Tenon to take us back to earth in his star-ship of light, during this light festival. (Christmas1985)

As can be seen from this communication, other aspects of divinity are often brought into specific space visualization journeys. The following communication was given by Arch Angel Aureal on the 7/11/83; once again I will only select parts of his communication because some have already been covered in other chapters of this book. ***There are other solar systems in this galaxy,*** (our milky-way) ***that have physical life on them; this life is also evolving, but not like earth, your earth evolvement, is special. Your galaxy is one of the youngest in this universe, but there are other galaxies that are younger, but as yet un-manifest. Let us enter our space craft, and go inwards towards Mercury - which cannot support life physically, and cannot be inhabited...... As we pass look at the satellites around it. Let us land on Mercury; see those building and space craft, they are etheric/physical. Now look back at your earth, you will see it is wobbling; the energies to stabilize earths wobble, come from Mercury.***

Let's go into that building - a miniature world, see the animals, birds, and other beings - who look different from us, they come from other planets. This is an exotic world with artificial lighting; the lighting comes from the forms that are here. Let us enter that observation tower.... *I have difficulty with your human forms here* please excuse me. We are waiting for those who use their minds to stabilize Earth, we are waiting for you to use your minds to help us. From this observation tower, technical (telepathic) ***information is channelled to earth, to assist their fellow man. You will see that there are two searchlight objects on this tower, beaming energy to earth; one is directed at the North Pole and one to the South Pole. A time comes when a spark will occur between these poles, and the earth's crust will shift. This spark will stabilize the earth wobble; please do not be fearful, because once this occurs, the true purpose and future of your earth, will unfold.***

When earth's crust moves, many will leave their earth bodies, returning to the astral planes; a few will survive the shift, and others might be uplifted by us, others still would be advanced initiates, and Ascension will occur, which is a quantum leap forwards. Mercury is a great mechanical workshop - a dynamo, sending our energy pulsations,(rays) *to your solar system. We are able to travel to our planets on these rays - in the etheric, by thought. The speed of light is boringly slow, as a means of travel; you must relearn the mechanics of transmutation..... to be able to ray travel within your solar system, then you will re-familiarize yourself with it, and also the star-gates, that you came in on. You have forgotten much of your spiritual being-ness, and ability; you will tarry awhile enthralled on your planets..... we will take you to them.*

A great space city is anchored at Alpha Centauri, and smaller craft visit your solar system from it - going to Jupiter or Mercury, the larger space cities, cannot come into your solar system, because of gravity; even in the etheric. If they did, there would be strong vibrational ripples that would affect human life, so we send scout ships - which have been seen in your skies, they are now ready to land, and are controlled from Mercury. They will land in desolated places to communicate with man, on a level that is not too infantile; three of these craft are ready to make contact with earth in the next three days or so. They must be meaningful contacts, not emotional, sensational, or of idle curiosity. There are energies on earth that would seek to stop us contacting you, let's harmonize and sterilize them.

From our observation point in this tower, we can see three places on earth - scintillating places; we need channels of light in these places - a triangulation, so that the brotherhood , the Bai'nor, can communicate with you at mental levels, in light, and love. Let us return to Earth..... see the fleets of men and angels, and our three doves of peace. (The three scout ships)*In the name of the Adonai, the Yodge Vodge, and archangel Michael, our love goes to earth and becomes a part of it. So be it... Thank you, Aureal.*

The reader will begin to understand the vastness of our true spiritual origins and being-ness. There is so much more that I could share with the reader from the Arel tapes but it would require separate books being written, so, sufficient unto the moment.

(* Aureal was having difficulty bringing the group's vibration up to that of Mercury.)

Chapter 11

I AM THAT I AM

SHAMBALA, (The New Jerusalem) and The Misty Isles (England).

Throughout the Arel tapes, frequent mention has been made about 'the misty Isles' in relation to earth spirituality, and discipleship training, during the last 15,000 years. The misty Isles of England and Ireland, were visited by divine teachers many times, to impart the ancient wisdom teachings. The early Celts and Druids knew that a great future lay in store for the tribes of these islands, and that they were to become the recipients of the light of truth. Because these islands were relatively isolated from the rest of Europe, it was hoped that these teachings would be kept pure.

Sadly - as with many tribal/ethnic groups, the deeper truths became distorted, and would eventually become lost over time. As so often happens, it was necessary for new teachers to incarnate into the isles of Albion, to reactivate the light centres, and the ancient wisdom teachings. Of fairly recent note are; Merlin, Boadicea, Milton, Shakespeare, William Blake, Isaac Newton, to name a few. These teachers were of Adamic en-condiment, and had many incarnations in the mystery temples of other lands and tribes such as; the Hindu's, ancient Egyptians, the red Indians of North America, the Tibetians, etc, To the spiritual hierarchy they were known as the 'Royal family', and would eventually incarnate into the tribes of Judah, and Palestine. The promised land of **ISRAEL** derives its name from; **IS** - the goddess Isis, **RA** - the Sun god - Sanat Kumar, and **EL** - the Elohim. Trained teachers from other lands would be drawn to incarnate into the Arab races, and Egypt; Moses was one of them, and had many prior incarnations in Egypt - including that of pharaoh.

William Blake's words to Jerusalem are, in my opinion, a searching insight about Jesus' visit to England, but more importantly, ascension. The Bible makes frequent reference to the New Jerusalem in relation to the so-called end times. The reader will now understand that the New Jerusalem, and Shamballa, are synonymous. Jerusalem - the etheric city of light, took responsibility for the experiment of earth, and the race of man, at the onset of the experiment. Shamballa is the place from which 'Gods' - ascended masters /Avatars, appeared to mankind throughout earth.

Many prophesies have been made about the re-appearance of the New Jerusalem, and some misinterpretation as well. Will the new Jerusalem/Shamballa actually materialize somewhere on earth, or is it just an analogy? William Blake had deep spiritual knowingness when he wrote the words to Jerusalem; it seems that he was directly in touch with the brotherhood of light, because much of his poem is part and parcel of the teachings on our tapes. We now know from channelled information that Jesus did indeed come to England as a boy, which supports William Blake's suggestion. It seems to me, that much of Blake's poem, are pointers towards Ascension;

Bring me my bow of burning gold - transmutation/Alchemy?

Bring me my arrows of desire -The arrow of Sagittarius, pointing to the cosmos?

Bring me my spear, Oh clouds unfold - The sword/spear of Archangel Michael, clearing the astrals?

Bring me my chariot of fire - Our Ascended light body?

I will not cease from mental fight, nor shall my sword sleep in my hand, till we have built Jerusalem in England's green and pleasant land.

In April 1993, John the Baptist gave this information about the masters Jesus' visit, to England; ***Yes, the young master Jesus was a frequent visitor to our house..... we were close family friends, and frequent visitors to the Essene communities, in the desert.***

(Amy; Beloved one did Jesus come from a poor family?) ***No, they were comfortable. Joseph earned a good living as a carpenter, and they were close friends of Joseph Tecurio - the Aramathean, indirect family. Joseph was appointed by the Romans to look***

after their interests in the area of Judea called Aramathea; he was highly thought of by the Romans, even though he was also in the Sanhedrin council. You know that he had mining interests in the misty Isles? (Yes) ***He made regular visits to that green and misty land; he took the young master with him on one such visit - they went via Carthage. The young master's feet walked on that soil.***

(Amy; Jesus, beloved one?) ***Yes the young master Jesus, he was about 11 years of age at the time of his visit.***

During a reading of chapter 133 of the Aquarian gospel, the Master Jesus came through, to give further insight into his time in England; once again I have only taken extracts from his communication, which came through in January 1998. ***Surely goodness and mercy shall follow me all the days of my life, and I will dwell in the house of the lord forever - in the soul forever. That is the meaning of the ending, of the 23rd psalm.***

(Amy reading from the Aquarian Gospel); They entered every village in Samaria, and preached in Tyre, and in Sidon; some went to Crete, and others into Greece, and others went to Gilliad to talk) ***Yes, and of course into the misty isles. They were sent by Joseph - the Aramathean - whose home was not too far away from Samaria itself, with the message of what was being revealed in Judea. These two, whom Joseph sent out, went with his own transport, his own ship and caravan, directly to the British royal family, or house.***

The message of the Kingdom was first established in that land, before any other. It was rejected in the land of its origins and by Rome, but in Britain - which had not come under the sway of Rome, the news of the kingdom was brought, and a centre point of light, was established. The first Christian church - although they did not call themselves that, was established in Glastonbury. That was the first place that the message of the kingdom, was established on the Earth of man; and there were a number of us who were familiar with those green hills. After the cosmic drama (his crucifixion and resurrection)***, many went back to their lands to take the message of the kingdom; you***

may still see differences in your various Christian churches, as to how the message was interpreted.

It is such a pity that the reader cannot hear the voice of the Master talking; a being of such incredible humility, and love, not to mention a wry humour. John the harbinger, (the Baptist) gave this communication on the 30/1/1986, revealing deeper insights, into the importance of Glastonbury, before the time of Christ, as a vibrant spiritual, earth grid vortex; ***The Jerusalem of ancient times, was your city of Shamballa. Your New Jerusalem will appear in Shamballa, but it will also appear once again, on the ancient temple sites of your planet. It was for that reason, that you were asked to go to Glastonbury,***(George and Amy visited Glastonbury in the early 80's) ***which is one of them.***

It is in Glastonbury that the New Jerusalem - for the new dispensation, will be built. John too was in that holy place at a time when the pure teaching of those you call the Druids, were taught..... *Astoria Hemanus* - the harbinger, the preparer of the way. Let us bless this centre of light and all those who guide your world at this time, and the times which lie within your experience, and your footsteps in light, and the planet. Shalom and Shalom.

ATOMS - Prana/Light/God.

The Atom - in relation to Ascension, are in truth part and parcel of the same thing. I have stated in this book that the source of our I AM body of light, began when the first spiritual atom - the act of first cause, manifested in the void. Beyond this - and more importantly, is the fact that we are divine consciousness; by transmutation, the first spiritual atom changed into an etheric atom, and finally - from let there be light, it transmuted into the physical atom, and thereafter, the physical Universes formed.

Much information came through over the years, in relation to form and the spiritual atom; this information would require a separate book being written, but I have taken extracts from the different tapes, as a means of giving divine mind explanations, to this complex subject, so here goes:

AREL; ***Love is the core essence of creation, it lies amongst the protons, and electrons of everything and everyone. Love is god, because man is the focal point of god. When they split that little thing, there are other things going around, and around. As a man thinketh IN - in other words, god is in all things.***

JOHNNY - 19/1/78: ***As a man thinketh in his heart, so is he, because man, is the focal point of god. As a man thinketh, so I AM is in man; right inside, even at the centre of your little atom and Nuclei, that keep going round and around.***

PER HOR; ***Lucifer's days are numbered. The prodigal son is the story of creation, it's about enlightenment. The tiny little atom - the proton entering into the vastness of its universe, contacts the electron, forming the whole, around the nucleus is the soul going forth, experiencing incarnation, and returning to our pure spiritual form.***

AVON - Aug 02; ***There is no difference between a grain of sand, and man! A grain of sand has a Shakinah body, and a feeling body; seven bodies, like your chakras, and an emotional body, like god. All is god - which is the source, penetrating every photon, and electron of creation, there is only god. Upgrade your consciousness! God has a uniquely personal contact, with every atom that he has created. I and my father are one!***

JESUS - Aug 87; (Amy was reading from the Aquarian gospel - Chapter 125, verse 21, as follows. I came in flesh to do the will of god, and lo this flesh and blood, are filled with Christ) ***Yes!.... I declared myself then as the Christos, which means the being filled with the Christos. Every atom of my physical form was Christ manifest, and therefore it was perfection. It could thus - even the physical self, move inter-dimensionally, because each Atom, was alive with the light of the Christ.***

ARCH ANGEL GABRIEL – 30/8/84;***Soul mind is the virgin spirit, which is the Christ. You can build a new world around you, by visualizing it into manifestation; it's like putting your whole planet under a cosmic microscope, and then magnifying it, until the particles of form, separate into cellular entities. Atomic particles - if magnified, become swirling vortices of***

energy; herein lies the truth of transmuting your physical form, into light, like Jesus did.

JOHNNY - 14/11/02; ***Life is in a state of constant fury, a state of eternality, infinity, and evolution. You cannot measure material substance. The smallest Atom in materiality is in a state of constant turmoil, change, and flux.***

ARCHANGEL AURIAL - 9/12/83;***The kingdoms of earth and mankind, are now awakening to a new energy, and vibration, an activation of the atom, and electron, and even the beings, within the electron.***

JESUS;***I told them I would remain three days in the tomb, in sweet communion with the Christ; with the father god, the mother god, and then symbolic of the ascent of the soul to higher life, my flesh within the atoms, would disappear. They would be transmuted into a higher from, and in the presence of all of them, I would ascend to god.***

RA AB HOUTEP - 28/9/95; (Dr: When ascension is achieved will the body be the same, if it is not perfect?) ***No! The atom is perfect therefore transmutation will purify and make perfect, any physical problems. The atomic seed thought is perfect.***

(Amy; If we do not achieve ascension, is it a failure?) ***The atomic structure of your body is perfect. Your physical bodies return to their perfect etheric atoms, and elements. The seed thought atoms of your body, are etheric/spiritual, therefore perfect. Your physical atoms are temporary, and may have imperfections in them from past life dis-ease, or Karma, but that is only physical. The seed thought from the mind of god is perfect, so the etheric atom is also perfect. AS ABOVE, SO BELOW.***

JOHNNY; ***Each atom, is a Deva vibrating. Chains of atoms are molecules vibrating at different levels. We ingest food that grew from the atoms of the soil, and the plant has its own atoms - the Devas. Your body is full of Devas, which are atoms. Love your body, your temple, and the Devas in it will respond with love, and then will your body be radiant. The atoms will vibrate at a higher level, and then as I be lifted up, so will I draw all men unto me.***

The master teacher Avon, gave this insight about the Christ and the atom, during a communication on the 11/11/02; ***When man leaves earth to return to the cosmos, he does so as the morning star of the Christ. The Christ is here - not Jesus of Nazareth, the Maitreya, the Imam Madi or any other leaders of spiritual paths; the Christ is that which IS, that which has never incarnated, can never incarnate into any form whatsoever, and yet paradoxically, that which is en-souled within the smallest atom of creation.***

ASCENSION, Transmutation, Alchemy, Transfiguration, and Resurrection.

Throughout the previous chapters, frequent information - some of it channelled, has been given about ascension and transmutation. By this stage, the reader will have a pretty good idea about the process necessary to achieve it. You will also have a better understanding of our divine being-ness, in that each and every one of us, is God/Goddess incarnate, therefore Omnipotent, Omnipresent, and Omniscient. Bearing this in mind, I offer the reader an overview of events that will almost certainly unfold in the very near future. I use the words almost certainly, advisedly, because our leap into cosmic consciousness lies squarely in our hands. By raising our consciousness - and all the kingdoms of Earth to unconditional love and light, ascension will occur as the prophesised 'New heaven and new earth'.

In July and August 1987, the master Jesus gave deep insights into chapter 127, verse 29 of the Aquarian gospel. Amy read as follows; (And then, symbolic of the ascent of the soul to higher life, my flesh within the tomb would disappear, it will be transmuted into a higher form, and in the presence of you, all I will ascend to God') ***Yes. I was preparing them for the fact that my human body would be destroyed - in the sense that it would be robbed of its life power, but even as a result of that, it would once again be resurrected through a consciousness that was pure, with the source. That would be the beginning of the teaching of the law, for the great new golden age that was to unfold, by transmutation of all substance, through the power of the mind divine, in man. My disciples still did not fully understand, or believe, that this frame***

of mine, would suffer death; I had tried to tell them, but they did not believe that I would not use the power that I had. I tried to convince them that my physical body was not the permanence of my being-ness, but what was important, was that through the demonstration of the law of transmutation, I could then bring man to a greater realisation of what his true essence really was.

Per Hor came through a number of times in the 70's and 80's, giving the group detailed information on Atlantis, Egypt, and other advanced early civilizations going back thousands of years. During one communication, he gave this beautiful information on ascension and transmutation; ***It is likely that some light channels will be lifted up by space craft, at the time of ascension. These craft are etheric so ascension will be an etheric experience. Animals will be part of ascension because their seed thought atoms are the same as yours.***

(Amy; Is ascension in the physical vehicle?)***Yes. By raising its vibration, it will transmute all your bodies into light. Many are receiving ascension training, in their sleep state. After ascension, you will be able to go into the worlds of thundering chaos, and create harmony, light, and life. Man's destiny is to create with his mind - and the fathers mind, forms, on other worlds; Galaxies, endless solar systems, and planets.***

Keep your vision beyond the stars, for you are eternal, immortal, and indestructible, children of the stars; you are star-seed incarnate. Continue to move forwards then, as the new race of Adam Kodman, (Ascended man)***for this is the vehicle for transmutation. You are a student of divinity, yet a ruler of matter in the lower world; this is man's unique place in creation, as student, and teacher. In the times before you, man will be in attunement with all of the lower kingdoms of nature, you are bringing to closure, your karmic link with earth forever. Your experiments in *Poside* and Egypt have brought you to the point that you are now at, the point of ascension, into cosmic freedom.***

Think on this; Jesus said, as I am so shall you be also, and thereafter, he transmuted his physical body into ascended consciousness, yet has appeared to mankind since that time, in

physical form. Your book tells you that man will don the wedding garment, which means that you are destined to ascend in your Shakinah body of light. By drawing divine love into your mind, it will enable you to transmute your lower vehicles, into light.

The physical form must be sacrificed voluntarily, to liberate the etheric form within you, so that you become an ascended cosmic being. Jesus said, what will you do when you see my blood transmuted into higher form? There will come a time, when each individual, will arrive at the point, where the great law of transmutation, will become enacted. Without preparation, how could they live in their new body of light; that is why it is so important, that man recognises that he is a body and being of light. When man realises that he is the incarnation of light, and love, then he will build for himself a pure Shakinah body of light; it is in that vehicle, that his consciousness will move, when the great law of transmutation is fulfilled.

Our ascended light body will be a blending of our physical, soul, and original spiritual body. Our soul's memory and experiences in creation and form, will become one with our ascended light body, incorporating all of our experiences, in all the kingdoms of nature, and with our fellow human beings, from past incarnations. It is important that we achieve ascension, because our ascended light body, and incarnate earth experiences, will enable us to be Greater than the angels. We will be recognised throughout the universes, as those special ones who underwent the experiment of embodiment in form. We will use our experience to raise the consciousness of life forms, on other planets.

Our new light body will be a wonder to behold, it will incorporate colours unseen anywhere in the universes. It will be a 'badge' of honour, for those special one's, who undertook the experiment of embodiment in creation, making us unique, and recognisable everywhere. What is man that thou art mindful of him, and the son of man, that thou visiteth him? The soul will be no more, for never again will divinity need to incarnate on physical planets, or into evolving species, in a lower vibrational soul sheath body, to carry out the will of the supreme creator, for we would have passed our tests!

The following extract from the Aquarian gospel of Jesus the Christ explains it this way; ***When man has conquered every foe upon the plane of soul, the seed will have fully opened out, it will have unfolded on the holy breath. The garb of soul will then have served its purpose well, and man will need it never more, it will pass and be no more. Man will then attain unto the blessedness, and perfectness, and be at one with God.***

On achieving ascension, we become ascended masters, one with the Avatar brotherhood. We will then be able - by thought and intention, to lower the vibrations of our ascended light body back into physical form, as Jesus did. We will take our earth experiences to other worlds and raise the consciousness of all form with compassion, understanding, and total knowingness of the difficulties that humanity has gone through. We may be looked at in fear by these other life forms - as we had done for many thousands of years during the experiment on earth, when gods had appeared before us. We may have to shout from the mountain tops to make the evolving species listen to us, but this time we will shout with love, and compassion, for we know what they are experiencing, because we did it, through thousands of years of evolution, birth, and death, in form. It was not by chance that the bible says; Ye are the goal of the gods.

TOWARDS ASCENSION - Unconditional love, forgiveness and service to our fellow man.

Each one of us has chosen our own unique spiritual or religious path, to truly understanding unconditional love. Unconditional love is divine love; in trying to achieve this, we must firstly strive to avoid judgment of others. We must love our fellow man unconditionally. (not an easy task considering the years of unloving, and judgmental conditioning, we have gone through, during our many embodiments) Before we can love our fellow man, we must first be able to truly love ourselves - a difficult thing to do because we know of the many unloving actions and thoughts perpetuated by ourselves to others. Unconditional love becomes more complicated when we try to understand and clear our unfulfilled karma from past lives. Unconditional love does not mean handing out flowers or telling everyone you love them; it means that in every situation you radiate love from your, I AM presence - in detachment.

If we do not forgive ourselves, then how can we truly forgive others? From a human mind perspective, unconditional love is not the easy way to enlightenment, but **it is the only way.** The divine truth of our I AM being-ness, and our love/wisdom, oneness with god, is the first principle of our spiritual vehicle of light, therefore the only way homewards! We must strive to get our human mind out of the way, realising and accepting, that it has been necessary for us to err on earth, in order that we could learn by it, and then return to the light and be 'greater than the angels'. Swami says 'love all, serve all', and also, 'help ever hurt never' these are all aspects of unconditional love.

On one occasion - during a reading from the Aquarian gospel, Jesus went on to talk about now times, he said; ***We dare not turn back. We have been preparing for these times, for many ages, and lifetimes, especially for the times that we find ourselves in, now. We are working with total planetary energies, as a new dispensation comes to birth, with the transforming energies of total and TOTAL transformation. When the result of this message had been grasped by my friends, and my beloved disciples, and you - and then by those who will follow you, in centuries to come, at that point will the earth experience, be completed. We are initiating the final phase of the plan of god for man upon this planet. That is why we are here. That is why the Christos en-souled my consciousness bringing together all the golden truths, the philosophies with the simple word LOVE. Now is the time for you to go forth as a teacher of the light, for all the knowledge of the world is worthless, unless you live Love.***

When Jesus told his disciples that he would be leaving them, they said; ***'Master what shall we do when you are gone?'*** and Jesus responded ***'Love one another as I have loved you, with all your heart, all your mind, and all your soul'*** It matters not whether the reader is a Christian, or follows other doctrines or faiths, only, that we are compassionate, considerate, caring and love-filled, towards our fellow man. Try to see beyond the anger, and aggression, that others perpetuate against you, radiate love from the secret place of the most high love and wisdom within you; it has been given that love radiated to a person, or situation, may receive a less than kind response; '***but that is not important, because what you send out in unconditional love, is always received. It might not be received by the human mind, but the soul always receives it, and gives thanks for it, because the soul always receives the message'.***

Strive to be detached in unloving situations in the divine knowingness that; '***Detachment doesn't mean a lack of caring. View what you are seeing or experiencing from a higher perspective, and surround it in unconditional love. Don't become involved in the emotion, just be still, and know that I AM, is god'.***

And what of the kingdoms and Earth? 'All things bright and beautiful the lord god made them all'; Try to remember that we are responsible for all earth kingdoms, and that they will also be raised to a higher evolutionary vibration, with us. Keep in mind the prophecy of the new heaven, and new earth, and our reasons for undertaking the experiment in the first place. On ascension we will lift up every atom within every kingdom - indeed the very earth itself, to a new position in the cosmos.

Within nature is a special stillness, a pulsating physical and etheric life force and energy. Ever have these kingdoms been there in service to man; indeed we have ingested them into our physical bodies for thousands of years, often without thought, or appreciation and rarely with love! The Devic kingdoms are now fighting back, because of our lack of appreciation of them, and the earth generally. This, together with other factors, is partly the reason for increasing floods, fires, earthquakes and cyclones. Give thanks, and love, to all earth kingdoms, when you ingest them into your body. Quietly tell a flower, or a tree of your love and appreciation for it because within the stillness of nature lies unconditional love.

In one of his early communications, Ra Ab Houtep spoke of the future of humanity and earth. I have taken a few extracts from his communication, which came through on the 16/3/1978; ***A time approaches when you will see yourselves wearing different garments, wearing different bodies –forms.... and speaking in different tongues...... as different nationalities. You will be*** *intrigued, because each one of you sees his own pattern.... and down through the ages, you hear the sound of the Ohm, it is this that ever brings you back to your awareness of your true home and self.*

You look forwards, and will see a time when, no longer can the writhing earth in torment, remain at the same vibration in its growth and evolution; and then it is - after many lifetimes of experience, you say father, may I return please, because I have seen the light of eternal truth. This is where you are now my children - channels of eternal light, still not understanding your great destiny...... and the powers that you have in you to create.

The days draw upon you, perhaps, when your world will no longer survive as you know it and see it, so do not be dismayed; do you not have within you the knowledge of the perfect plan of god and his creation in man..... you have seen it! You have seen the days that lie before you in your earth experience that has yet in your time and space, to come to you. Their lies before you in the door that lies open now, the land of promise..... enter through the door. The time when the golden dispensation of man shall appear in the mists, is now with you, it's here!

It may be that the vibration of the earth will no longer be able to hold the light of a new age..... and the crust of the earth may shatter..... and form - as you know it, may disappear, revealing the true, and new, and eternal you. When the master Jesus stepped forward from the tomb - on that Easter morning, he said, do not touch me..... for I am not yet transcended - you may say the word ascended, if you wish.

Be not dismayed at what is taking place in your world scene, it is not destruction, it is re birth..... it is not terror, it is joy that the eternal is to come to the consciousness of man, and his planet. For those of you in your physical bodies, you shall at no time lose your consciousness..... you shall go on to greater glory. Speak with Ra Ab Houtep, if you wish.

(Amy: beloved one the Christ that has come down through the ages, could you speak on that please) ***Yes, the Kristos..... the holy spirit, the new body of the new earth, that is the Christ. Just as the master Jesus transmuted his body of flesh into the body***

eternal, so shall the world of man - his gross world, be transmuted into the body eternal, in the twinkling of an eye. As your sins be as scarlet, they shall be washed as white as snow, these things are in your scriptures. These are days of singing, dancing, and rejoicing, and..... Man is the vessel that contains the Christ..... does that answer your question? (Thank you yes.)

Towards ASCENSION - Energy follows thought.

When the human mind and the divine mind are linked by the rainbow bridge - the Antekarana bridge, our soul mind is able to impress our human minds, thereby reminding us, that we are creator beings of light. It has been said so many times in this book, and the entities who have given us the ancient wisdom teachings, that Energy follows thought, therefore what you give your attention to, can or will manifest. This creative thought energy, go's out from us at human, and soul mind levels, and something always happens!

Simeon once said***; There is another governing factor, and this is what is facing all man at the moment. Whatever man shall give his attention to will manifest for him. If you concentrate on any one thing, you will give it power to exist, to grow, and to become perfect; should that thought be negative, then your thoughts create something that will master you, and if you thought create something positive, it will be used as a tool to bring forth enlightenment. Whatever the mind of man shall concentrate on, will manifest, it is inevitable, it cannot be changed, for it is the law of creation. Ultimately, man was to demonstrate that so powerful was the mind, that it would have complete control over the physical body, through the process known as death. Do you understand these things, if not please say so. If a man gives attention to his imperfections, those very imperfections are given the power to live! Think on that one.***

So we create our own reality, therefore give your attention to the perfect manifestation of god within you. 'I if I be lifted up will draw all men unto me'; the master Jesus said these words, because he came to show man that we are divine sparks of god. 'As I am, so shall ye be also', is what he told his disciples, when appearing before them after his ascension. He also said 'Things that I do you can do and even greater things'. Even though his body was physically dead on the cross, he raised his body from death into ascended consciousness, promising mankind that we can do it, then added; 'It is the father within that doeth the works'.

We must learn to let go and forgive ourselves, and others, taking strength from the fact that his disciples were still squabbling amongst themselves for Jesus' attention, right up until the 11thhour, as to who was more worthy, or should occupy the seat next to him, at the last supper. Strive to forgive yourself, and others, and that energy will go out in thought, to the corporate mind of man. We can change the world, or add to its miseries, the choice is ours. Many of us give attention to human emotional sadness, judgment or anger, on what we hear, or see on TV programmes. Chain letters, threatening us with dire consequences if we do not pass them on, or a web site that might ask you to sign up and express your anger, at this regime, or that cause, all add to negative thoughts going out as energy. I hope it is now apparent that our thoughts and judgments to negativity in any form merely adds to it. The reverse is also true; strive to see these events for the illusions that they really are in relation to our godhood, and from that perspective, that we can change the world!

Wherever starvation, suffering, and pain occur in drought stricken areas, we question a merciful god and ask, why is god is so cruel; by focusing on the suffering, and pain, we add to it, and then that energy goes out into the corporate mind, creating more sadness and pain. We can - as incarnate gods, visualise rain falling in that country; see the rivers flowing, the grass growing, and the people happily planting seeds. Call on the Devic kingdoms, thanking them for nurturing the crops of your visualisation, and thought creation, this really works, believe it! Raise your hands where you see cruelty to animals, or others, then visualize light, Swami, Jesus, or Mary, or whoever, within that situation, and hand over. Hand over and say, 'thy will be done on earth as it is in heaven'. Many books, tapes, CD's, etc, are available to the reader, and some can be downloaded from the web. The metaphysical scientist Gregg Bradon or Ekhart Tolle, both explain in great detail the power of thought, and intention, and are really worth reading, or listening to.

ASCENSION - Realized?

And now I stick my neck out, in trying to explain to the reader what has come to me during meditations, insights, and clear dream recalls. These insights have occurred during the past 60 years, and may already have changed. I see a time rapidly approaching, when the brotherhood of light will transmute their vast etheric star-ships of light into form, and the whole of humanity will behold these beautiful craft in the heavens. They will emit a calm vibrational sound to earth, which will ease the mind of many who will suddenly realize that 'God' has come for their redemption. Some of humanity will be in fear, whilst others might be guided to sit quietly by themselves; others still will be drawn strongly to the nature kingdoms, and remote unspoilt areas. Within the stillness of nature, or their homes, they will suddenly become aware of unconditional love, or a state of meditative peace. An open etheric doorway may appear before some of us; some will step through without fear, or doubt. We will see the smiling faces of our loved ones, or our guardian angels, who will joyously take our hand and say, welcome home, our beloved brother/sister of light.

I see many craft in the skies; some are moving and some are stationary. I see their shapes; some are different from the others.... an arrowhead formation, an ovoid formation, and vast sun discs. During the day time, I see these craft clearly, they are vast and awe inspiring, and there is a pattern, or writing on some of them. Of a night, their lights are magnificent, and very bright; some people will fear them and others will have an innate knowing about them, but many will not understand what they really mean. Some of the world powers will try to intercept them with their technology - but if threatened by the planet of angry gods, they will de-materialise, causing confusion and fear. Some of our enlightened friends, and family, will simply disappear before our eyes; young children will be absorbed into their parents ascension energy, and will be 'lifted-up' with them. I see a period of a few weeks - but cannot be sure of the timing, when all volcanic activity, and earth movements, cease, as vast beams of unseen energy from Sirius, the Zodiac houses, and the biospheres of light, stabilize earth and calm returns.

I see Angels and teachers moving amongst groups of semi-enlightened people, who will suddenly 'see the light', because they will be in the energy and vibration of these teachers and Avatars, and will be assisted to ascend. 'The stars will appear to fall from the skies' as our solar system moves into the new heaven, nearer the Pleiades. Those not of the light, will strive to keep the old order of judgement, and anger, and try to control humanity. Some will be under the control of the negative powers, but not for long, for the new earth will be reborn into light.

The following communication by Avon, came through on the 3/10/1985; ***Earth is but a training school. A time fast approaches, now when you will be moving into a new experience of consciousness, as a planet, and solar system. Your Solar system is entering a null void zone, which means it will be transported to another corner of this vast universe, in which it presently revolves.***

(Dr; Will it be going along another upwards spiral?) ***Yes, it will spiral to a place that has been vacated by another solar system, which is more advanced than your own. As the great sun of Kolob, separates the mazzaroth, so do universes, and galaxies, move with that opening...... You will be ascending into a state of light; you will be evolving, you can search your scriptures, and if you have the eyes to see and the inner ear to hear, you will see that what Avon is saying, was revealed to your ancient sages.***

You will be moving into your Merkabah vehicle of light, and taking yourself with it, (our human form) ***in your Shakinah body of light - not merely individually, but as a solar system. At present, your experience could be described as blind flying, because your vision is limited by the denseness of your solar experience. Your material form, can only receive a small amount of cosmic radiation, otherwise it would be destroyed; so your form has to be transmuted, in order for you to enter into the consciousness of a light vehicle, do you understand? It is quite exciting, but prior to all this activity, certain fulfilments have to be undergone, you have to equate much of your earth experience under the great cosmic law of balance,*** (Karma) ***do you have any questions?***

(Amy; We have been told that the cosmic Christ, will en-soul the solar Christ in the sun, and then all vibration will radiate outwards, is this what you are talking about?) ***It is just that indeed. The cosmic Christ,*** (Sai Baba) ***is the en-soulment of the Sun of Kolob, which will then en-soul the Sun of your solar system, and others, in a greater evolution. The whole of the mazzaroth of Kolob, is in the process of spiralling to a greater light. What is transpiring now, is that by your conscious attunement with the great principals of love, and light, you are building for yourselves finer light bodies. Some of you will desire to enter into the spiritual realms - some of you here present, others desire to do that, and also explore your mazzeroths, etheric/physical worlds.***

Some individuals on your planet will enter our craft in their physical form - there are those who desire to do so, others will enter into their light bodies, and move beyond the mazzaroth, into the greater paradise worlds of the father. There are others still, who by the action of their lives - their embedded consciousness and crystallisation in materiality, will choose to be taken to other planets, and star worlds. Ultimately of course, all will evolve to light.

Throughout our bible, are many references to the Mazzeroth star houses, some of which are; the gate-ways of Orion, Arcturus, Alpha Centauri, the Pleiades, etc. (see Job Chapter 9 - V9; Job chapter 38 – V31; and other places) It is given in revelation's, that in the end times, 'the stars will fall from the sky'. (Revelations chapter 6 verse 13) Prophecy is indeed interesting for it seems that our solar system will leave the photon belt, and will be drawn into the gravitation pull of the great sun of Alcion, in the Pleiades. Indeed it will seem that the stars will fall from the skies, but this might not be seen by human eyes, or will it? Nine hundred years ago, the Druid mystic Merlin, spoke of a time when 'the planets will run riot through the signs'. I believe he was referring to the signs of our 12 Zodiac houses. John (the disciple) says; the graves will open, and those semi-enlightened ones who left earth prior to these times, can return to take a tiny atom from the form that they once occupied, to become ascended masters.

Those not of the light who spent their last life time as manipulators, and controllers of mankind, and live for domination, wealth, and possessions, will be given the choice of another planet, where they will have to learn their lessons all over again. They will be bound to that planet, for a thousand years. 'We will wait patiently for them to return to us, for they are in truth our brothers, and sisters, of light. When they return to the realms of light, there will be no judgment; they will be welcomed home, in unconditional love'.

There are still many parts of the jigsaw missing in relation to ascension, transmutation, and the future of our Earth. Many years ago Swami indicated that he will leave earth in 2012, and return as Prema Sai - SUPREME LOVE in 1918; Swami actually left his body on the 17th of April 2011, for reasons known only to him. One entity prophesys that a great teacher will incarnate into the indigenous race in Southern Africa, and will be a great way-shower for the world as a whole. This information is most interesting, in view of what was given to the Arel group about Rhodesia and Southern Africa many years ago.

The timing of ascension is unknown to anyone, Johnny once said; ***The time is known to no one, not even the master Jesus. It will come like a thief in the night; two will be working in the field, and suddenly one will disappear, just like that.*** Earth's new position in the galaxy will be a stepping off point for ascended man to create, and teach, throughout the cosmos of creation. Just prior to ascension, man and women of earth will indeed ***'talk in tongues'*** because our consciousness would have risen to divine knowingness to such an extent, that we will recall all our many incarnations, and the various languages that we spoke during them. RAH gave this information, in a communication that came through, on the 10/3/78; ***You will see your lives flashing by before you, as if they were drawings on a wall. You see yourself doing strange things, sometimes - often indeed, together, and sometimes apart; wearing different garments, bodies and forms, and speaking in different tongues, as different nationalities.***

Avon took the group on a visualization visit to Spica - in the Zodiac house of Virgo, and then handed over to Archangel Gabriel who spoke about the future of earth in relation to ascension, and transmutation. 30/8/84***; May the plan of the creator manifest itself through you. Do not be afraid, have no fear and know that*** *you are held in the palm of his hand; no matter what might transpire in the illusionary life that you pursue, in this your illusionary world, you are in the palm of his hand. No ill can come to you, unless you allow it to; accept all the experiences that your lives offer you, and then hold them up to the crystal of pure light and truth, and see for yourself, their true value.*

It has been said to you 'except a man be born again he cannot enter the kingdom of heaven'. Many times indeed, has your consciousness known birth, and rebirth, in the physical body and vehicle of man; during these times it has known birth, death, and rebirth, under the laws of the lower heavens - the great Karmic law of, 'as ye sow so shall ye reap'. You are no longer bound by the worlds of flesh, and matter. When next you incarnate your consciousness - if you so desire, it shall be that you initiate a move through the attainment of the purity within, as a reborn Christ child, instead of returning under the law of the lower heavens. You can build for yourself a Shakinah body, and a Merkabar vehicle, of permanence.

The following message can only be described as incredibly beautiful, and worth sharing with those on the path of light. It was given by the Master Jesus on Christmas day, 1990; ***Blessings and greetings. All love, joy, peace on earth, and goodwill to all men. From the inner planes of light, there is a great company of light beings descending towards man's earth. All the goodwill and love, which rises on this day, will be gathered like precious gems. Channels of light from ages past are now incarnate in man's world and have been prepared for these days. - And now is the time of fulfilment. Many have been the ways in which the light has manifested in the consciousness of man; many have been the leaders who have come to him, and many have been the paths that he has followed.***

All these ways, leaders, and paths, have now converged, for man is consciously becoming a whole, upon this earth of his. With that wholeness, you will develop a sense of interdependence and brotherhood; from that, will grow a love, of one for the other. Like beacon lights, great souls will stand in the portals of eternity in relationship to man's world; great ones

who have given their all for the up-lift-ment of mankind into his spiritual being – his soul awareness, have come, with their many helpers down through the ages of time, and they now walk amongst man himself.

From the planetary centre of your hierarchy have come great beings into the earth of man, once again. They walk with man to teach him of love, and of the permanence of that relationship between himself, and god, and himself and himself, with god as the link. There is only one message that comes to man in these days, love one another, as I have loved you. Man has gone through all of his experimentations...... he has inflicted his brutalities one upon another, and has become dead in his soul, in the earth of man. So a cry has gone forth, 'lord hear our prayer, let our cry come unto thee', and it is now answered. At last many of man, are putting behind themselves the things of earthly value, and casting aside those things which have separated him - one from another, holding him in bondage, in the worlds of matter.

Let us in this time, join, in throbbing love, and fellowship, and enter the portals of eternity. Come my brothers and sisters, let us walk together in joy, and love; let us smile together, let us laugh together, let us dance together, and let this be the total reality of the new age, as we now enter into it. Let us open wide the doors behind us so that our brothers and sisters, may follow with us. Let there be no more closed doors and shut windows. Let us walk on the open highways of life and into eternity; those of you who celebrate this day, with all the magic and wonder of love that comes with it, blessed be you. Let your heart sing through it, as you know that it is one of the countless days of eternity, which lie before you. The shadows fall away from you as you step into the light and no longer acknowledge the darkness...... Behold, the day-spring from on high has visited us, so be it. Blessings and greetings my beloved ones, my beloved companions, my beloved brothers, and sisters.

Detachment

Letting go from all that binds us to the earth scene is a very difficult area that we must come to terms with, and will assist us in the ascension process, because the emotions and feelings of human life, and love, are very binding to the physical universe. Detachment doesn't mean lack of caring or lack of love for our families and friends, It means that we must work at being able to stand back from situations, and emotions, in the full knowingness that we are Eternal Immortal and indestructible beings of light. What transpires in our life is an illusion to what we truly are. Were we not one with the supreme creator in the beginning, and did we not choose our embodiments on earth for perfect reasons, and latterly to equate Kharma, and thereby reach a quantum understanding that we are more than our human body, and mind?

Considering the many communications from divine mind in this book, we know that each one of us is a divine being of light - be it a child or a 90 year old person, in lesson on earth by our own desire, to do the father's will on Earth as it is in heaven. A beautiful sensitive three year old child is in truth a trillion year old Angel, who joyously came to earth to learn, grow, and ultimately to take its experiences back into other worlds of creation. We cannot judge what is right or wrong for our fellow man but we must guide and teach our children during their impressionable years, that love and compassion is the only way forwards for all of us, regardless of race, gender, etc. Never forget that, YOUR CHILDREN CHOSE YOU! TO BE THEIR PARENTS, in full soul knowingness and their reasons for incarnating, this time round.

Stand back from what occurs in the earth scene and project from your mind unconditional love, into every situation; if the situation becomes difficult, hand over to your higher self, or the avatar of love, and remember he sent his son to earth in the full knowingness of the potential outcome of 'His' will. Try to see beyond the histrionics, anger, and judgment in all interactions with your fellow man, for indeed it is an illusion to the truth of who we really are. Be detached in unconditional love.

Faith and trust

Prophesied entry into and through, the photon belt and the resultant earth movements because of it, will bring much confusion and fear to those who exist at a purely physical human mind level, but it must now be obvious that they are in a no win situation! Earth's full entry into the photon belt will be very different this time because it coincides with mass ascension; John's Revelation talks about a new heaven and a new earth, ***heaven and earth shall pass away but my word will never pass away.*** Humanity's state of raised consciousness to its divine truth has, to a certain extent, changed earlier predictions of doom and gloom as more and more of us wake up to our I AM presence.

This extract by GAN came through on the 24/12/04, and was entitled, Heavens ablaze; ***Gan is sending this communication out into the ethers… others are listening in. Great preparations are being made in the etheric mazzeroth to accommodate each individual consciousness who will be affected by the re-orientation of your planet and solar system.***

Gan would like to assure you that light channels will not experience violent transition….. for those who do not believe in violence…… but those who have willingly chosen the dark path there may well be psychological……. re-adjustments……. until such time as they choose to return to the path of the source.

There is no reason why any incarnate or discarnate individual should align themselves with anything less than the cosmic power of love and light and the creators presence and being; man has chosen to do this and has brought about, on the material and etheric levels, traumatic and dramatic situations…… in many instances climatic because many people seeing these things have had to reflect on the purpose of life.

We take this time to bring your attention to the wonderful concept of rebirth Earth. Great entities have incarnated into the very depths of darkness for these times…… knowing that whilst incarnate they would forget their celestial origins and commit acts which would…… perhaps…. set them back for many millennia were they not light beings. At great sacrifice they have chosen to be a light in the darkness… the darkness which your scriptures say comprehendeth it not…… but you light channels gird this planet in a ring pass not of light in order to

ensure that the experiment that you undertook, at the dawn of it, will not have to be repeated.

During these times you are very closely linked with your guides and brothers and sisters of light on the inner planes.... move forwards as you see fit and do the right thing as you see you should.... and don't waste time in trying to assess whether you are doing the right thing.

The words of that great hymn are very appropriate at this time....... 'Nothing in my hands I bring, only to thy cross I cling'.... this does not refer to a crucified Jesus. The cross is symbolic of crossing out the material to the spiritual so that two great pillars of light, like the pillars of Solomon's temple, will guide man in the future. Gan will not say more at this time even though he could, you are entering the final stages of your move into liberation.

Johnny – 28/7/95, Faith and trust

*I'd like to talk around two important subjects..... attachment..... or detachment, and the other one is the difficult business of Faith. As you know there is a tremendous descent to earth of light beings and waves of incoming illumination and love..... and most people seem to be waking up to it...... is that not so? (*no response) *Oh! You don't think they are!*

(Yes Johnny we do) *The times are unique because never before has there been a conscious awakening to the fields of spiritual exploration and enlightenment...... once again people are being faced with having to make a choice between what is intuitively right or instinctively what they know is wrong or expedient. Many who pass on or pass over from the physical into the inner planes instinctively cling to their senses of values and what they've learnt on earth..... many bring with them a warped sense of values because they regard everything from a material point of view.....like possessions, fame, human relationships, property owning, and all this kind of thing..... according to their attachment to these things they are held back, or soon liberated from them.*

Whatever inner plane world you move into is based on the ethics and morals you built around yourself during that last incarnation including all your values, and then you realize how short the credit side of your bank balance was. Faith….. put your faith into what you believe most deeply in your heart….. detach yourself from whatever situation you are in and hand over….. your right to decide what you are going to do with your life or your possessions. Have faith that the great power is going to provide you with everything that is necessary in order to complete the plan (the earth experiment and ascension) ***that you came into incarnation to fulfil. There is no thing and no one which is greater than god within you and that's the test point of faith….. but detachment is very important….. it doesn't mean that you've got to give up everything, only that you identify with everything from the point of view of the divine desire. Take the normal steps you have to but trust to the power beyond that, and the being-ness will take you through what you need to go through; you've got to have unquestioning faith and trust in god's plan for you and the world.***

(Amy; Johnny now is the last bastion of Christianity which the dark powers are working all out to smash….. the light) ***Yes….. your Swami is the reference point for those reaching for the god realization within, that is why the great divine has incarnated.***

(Amy; Johnny... concerning Swami….. a long time ago you told us to take your picture down that was hanging on the wall and now look what's happened (Amy was referring to the photograph I sent them of Swami which was hung where Johnny's photograph used to be)

Have faith and trust that a great power is rolling in on the shores of a new age, nothing can stop it.

(Dr; Johnny the photon belt is getting nearer or we are getting nearer to it or passing through it?) ***Well…. you should have been living in the Photon belt for quite a long time already,***

(Amy: Spiritually?) ***….. Where is the dividing line between spirit and matter?.... you see, you've got a point of view haven't you? You left yourself wide open for that one didn't you?*** (Laughter… Yes Johnny)

Have total faith and trust that the incoming power of light is so tremendous that nothing can stand in its way and all glory is ready for those….. who haven't yet found it. You need not be worried about anything; you know you cannot die and that you are god….. god is life, god is light, god is everything…… he hasn't got any place for anything dead in him .

Egypt revisited

In November 2007, I visited Egypt with a group of spiritually minded friends - Kim my future wife, and her son John, were also part of our group. A well planned but hectic tour of all the important temples had been arranged. I found the corporate human mind of Egypt very distracting - especially Cairo, but Luxor, and Aswan, were beautiful, despite tourist group leaders trying to out shout each other at the various temple sites. Our accommodation in Luxor provided a rooftop view which was very peaceful; I found myself sitting quietly most afternoons, looking towards the Nile, and the Valley of the Kings. We visited temples, from Abu Simbel in the South, to Heliopolis, (On) in the North. I developed very bad flu within four days of arriving, which eventually turned into Bronchitis, so I was a bit of a passenger, trying to keep up with everyone during visits to the various sacred sites, and temples.

Some days were spent sailing in a Felucca, and also a one day trip downstream, in a tourist boat to the temple of Edfu. The Nile was beautiful, but devoid of Egyptian geese, hippos, fish eagle, and crocodiles, which saddened me, having become accustomed to the incredible wildlife on the Zambezi, and Kafue rivers, and knowing that these species had been prominent in Egypt, up until recent times. I took some Arel tapes with me, but apart from two others in our group it was mainly our Bulawayo family who listened to them regularly. We had grown into en-lighten-ment with the Arel tapes years before, making it easier for us to understand, and relate, to the deep messages within them. We had a very short visit to what remains of On; sadly the group did not want to stay there, so we did not play the tape of the master Jesus which spoke about his revisit to On, and the Devic kingdoms.

Our visit to the pyramids of Giza was amazing, even though I found myself struggling to breathe, and keep up with everyone else. Our tour organizer - Julie, felt it was important for me to visit the Kings chamber in the great pyramid. I was unsure as my chest hurt, and I could not catch my breath. Kim, John and Amura-An went in, but I stayed behind. I sat on a stone at the base of the main pyramid whilst, they went for a walk to the second pyramid. Julie was waiting for me at a pre-arranged spot and handed me my ticket to the Kings chamber; it seemed that I was going in whether I thought I could make it or not. The second stairway upwards was proving difficult but I pressed on. Half way to the top, I stopped, gasping for breath. I thought I was going to pass-out and flopped down trying to get air into my lungs. I sat on the outer edge of the narrow stairway for about fifteen minutes trying to slow my heartbeat as everyone passed by. Eventually I crawled on all fours into the Kings chamber, flopping down on the floor with my back against the wall next to the Sarcophagus. It seemed my delayed arrival was perfect because there was no one else in the chamber. I sat quietly in meditative mood and eventually an Austrian man entered and sat down next to me. He told me that this visit was the fulfilment of his life's dream then went on to tell me about the red granite stone blocks that comprised the Kings chamber. After a while, we sat quietly and then I started intoning the Aum and he joined in with me. It was a special moment but then we heard voices of other tourist coming up the stairs so we just sat quietly together. The last few tail-enders came and went and then once again, the chamber was quiet.

The temple at Philae was incredible, and is where the lotus pool of Ra Ab Houtep and Per Hor, is located in the etheric. Everyone in the group were spiritually affected by Philae but, once again, I had difficulty with all the tourists and tour operators shouting out their stories. I know that many of the tourists had also been drawn to Egypt because of probable past lives there, but it was just so distracting. I remembered what it used to be like four to five thousand years ago; the sanctity, sacredness and peace of an era past.

It seemed there was nowhere I could go to connect to the ambiance of what I once knew existed in the ancient land of Khaam. Things were so much more genteel thousands of years ago; there was honour, respect and love manifest in so many important ways. Overall there was a sadness in me - a melancholic feeling, because of what ancient Khaam used to be - and what it is now.

We went to the island of Elephantine where I had an immediate connection. We went across to it on a felucca, and apart from a small excavation group, there were only four of us on the island. I was standing in Amen Houtep the 3rd's gateway when suddenly; A large brightly coloured reed boat approached the landing at the top of the island; a high initiate was sitting on a sun shaded dais…. attendants lazily fanning him. And then the vision was gone!

Our visit to Abydos was amazing and I now understand re-occurring dreams - or past life memories that have been with me throughout my life. These dreams relate directly to the sacred temple pond and the red granite pillars at the rear of Abydos. This water feature has been imprinted on my mind since childhood and I stood looking down at it in disbelief. John, Kim and I sat there for a long time and then John pointed out the flower of life symbol on the second pillar in the pond. Drunvello Melchizadek had spoken about this symbol as had others. I particularly recalled the Cartouches of all the Pharaohs in the temple and knew that I had been at Abydos a long time ago.

The energy at the step pyramid at Saqara was also very strong, and once again, I felt that I'd come home. Despite the madding crowd, we shared a taped message on the southern side of the pyramid. The tomb of the great advanced initiate priest Imen Houtep - now called Im Houtep, is still being looked for, but this will never be found, because he was one of the winged pharaohs, and according to our tapes, an ascended master (an Avatar). Im Houtep transmuted his body into light when his earth mission was completed.

Karnak - as has been given, was an important part of my priesthood initiation and I have already mentioned some hazy past life memories that have come back to me. Kim, my beloved friend and sister of light, stayed close by me as I wandered through the remains of Karnak. Much had changed; huge covered areas that once surrounding the holy of holies - the inner sanctum, have gone. I wandered around trying to locate my sanctuary of 2400 years ago; a large green marble entrance doorway got my attention, and then, the remains of the red/white marble statue of Isis. I said to Kim it has to be around here somewhere? I can feel the energy but much of the original structure has totally changed'. She smiled at me very calmly and I knew she was creating a sacred space around me to help me focus.

Close to the inner sanctum I stopped….. I was drawn to an area to my right. I said to Kim, it's here, this is it. We walked into a rectangular enclosure... Yes, this was the place! We sat in one of six alcoves that once held beautiful statues of Isis, Osiris, Horus and three other relatively unknown ancient Egyptian deities. The roof had gone and the remaining walls were only five feet high; the black marble stone slab had also gone but its plinth was still there - a sandstone plinth about four tons in weight. The size of this sanctuary was exactly right, about 30 meters long, 15 wide, with a raised 'stage' platform about 4ft high. Behind this were the remains of an old doorway, which led into my old living quarters. I was babbling on to Kim, as ancient visions, and memories kept coming back to me; bless her, she just sat quietly with me. On a wall next to the entrance door was the remains of a red granite font...... I remembered that it used to be held in the hands of a Cherub, but that was no longer there.

I wanted to climb onto the dais to locate my old room at the back, but a temple guard would not allow it. My flu, and chest infection, was starting to get better - having almost completed a course of antibiotics. Two mornings before we were due to fly back to the UK, I woke up with Johnny's voice ringing in my ears, he said; 'About your visit to Karnak....... you haven't quite got it right, but it will come to you, all is well, lo I am with you always'.

My return to England was one of mixed feelings concerning our visit to Egypt, because I had expected so much. Sadly, I had allowed the corporate human mind, to disconnect me from the real purpose of my visit. Others of our group, had their own connections with Egypt confirmed, in some way or another, but I seemed to be piggy in the middle. But then it changed about three days after our return to the UK; I started to have clear dream state recalls, together with a voice talking to me. I would wake up and hear ABYDOS.... ABYDOS, repeatedly - almost urgently, as if I was being reminded of something, or confirmation was being given? This happened for three nights in a row, and then about two days later, I woke up with a clear dream state recall of Saqqara;

To the west of Saqqara - between the pyramid and the temple site - and deep under the sands - are the remains of three initiate temples, the walls and roofs, long gone. The floor of each temple has nine large square slabs as its base; I see myself standing on one of these slabs in the first temple which is on the left, looking Westward's..... I am going through some initiate training process and, as I pass my tests, I step onto the next slab. I successfully completed temple one and two but woke-up as I was about to step onto the eighth slab of the last temple. The identical dream sequence and failure to continue onto the last two stones occurred for two nights in a row. Since then, I have had no further dream recalls of Saqqara.

(* I'm not sure of the spelling or pronunciation of Astoria Hemanus, or its meaning, but it seems that when John was at Glastonbury, he may have been known to the Druids, by that name.)

(* Poside refers to the last Atlantean dispensation, about 8,500 years ago.)

Lightning Source UK Ltd.
Milton Keynes UK
UKOW051225221111

182468UK00001B/1/P